A U T H E N T I
ARTS & CRAF
FURNITURE
P R O J E C T S

FROM THE EDITORS OF POPULAR WOODWORKING

POPULAR WOODWORKING BOOKS
CINCINNATI, OHIO
www.popularwoodworking.com

METRIC CONVERSION CHART

to convert	to	multiply by
Inches	Centimeters	2.54
Centimeters	Inches	0.4
Feet	Centimeters	30.5
Centimeters	Feet	0.03
Yards	Meters	0.9
Meters	Yards	1.1
Sq. Inches	Sq. Centimeters	6.45
Sq. Centimeters	Sq. Inches	0.16
Sq. Feet	Sq. Meters	0.09
Sq. Meters	Sq. Feet	10.8
Sq. Yards	Sq. Meters	0.8
Sq. Meters	Sq. Yards	1.2
Pounds	Kilograms	0.45
Kilograms	Pounds	2.2
Ounces	Grams	28.4
Grams	Ounces	0.04

Authentic Arts & Crafts Furniture. Copyright © 2000 by Popular Woodworking Books. Manufactured in China. All rights reserved. No part of this book may be reproduced in any form or by any electronic or mechanical means including information storage and retrieval systems without permission in writing from the publisher, except by a reviewer, who may quote brief passages in a review. Published by Popular Woodworking Books, an imprint of F&W Publications, Inc., 4700 East Galbraith Road, Cincinnati, Ohio, 45236. First edition.

Visit our Web site at www.popularwoodworking.com for information on more resources for woodworkers.

Other fine Popular Woodworking Books are available from your local bookstore or direct from the publisher.

07 06 05 04   8 7 6 5

Library of Congress Cataloging-in-Publication Data

Authentic arts & crafts furniture / by the editors of Popular Woodworking Books.
    p. cm.
  ISBN 1-55870-568-6 (alk. paper)
  1. Furniture making--Amateurs' manuals. 2. Furniture, Mission--United States--Amateurs' manuals. 3. Arts and crafts movement--United States--Amateurs' manuals. I. Title: Authentic arts and crafts furniture. II. Popular Woodworking Books (Firm)
TT195 .A98 2000
684.1'04--dc21   00-033633

Edited by Jennifer Churchill
Designed by Brian Roeth
Cover designed by Lou Beckmeyer
Cover photography by Robert M. Hale
Production coordinated by Emily Gross
Editorial assistance by Clara Ellertson

Page layout by Donna Cozatchy
Copyedited by Lisa M. Collins
Proofread by Kenya McCullum
Indexed by Brian Feil
Photography by Al Parrish

PROJECT AUTHORS

Christopher Schwarz, Senior Editor, *Popular Woodworking* magazine: Morris Chair, Limbert Two-Door Bookcase, Garden Storage Bench, Byrdcliffe Wall Cabinet, Cellarette, Limbert Wastepaper Box

Jim Stack, Associate Editor, Popular Woodworking Books: Limbert Inlaid Rocker

Bruce Stoker, contributor, Heirloom Quilt

Jim Stuard, Associate Editor, *Popular Woodworking* magazine. Greene & Greene Entry Bench, Greene & Greene Garden Bench, Greene & Greene Patio Table

David Thiel, Senior Editor, *Popular Woodworking* magazine: Box Spindle Chair, Spindle Side Table, Stickley Side Table, Roycroft Magazine Stand, Knockdown Bookcase, Bungalow Mailbox, Sideboard, Mantel Clock, Wright Hall Tree

Christopher Schwarz and **David Thiel**: Octagonal Taboret, Two Frames

Arts and Crafts furniture is one
of the most popular furniture
styles woodworkers want to build ... and an interest in
Arts and Crafts furniture can quickly turn into an addiction. *Popular Woodworking* magazine's senior editors have
formed such an addiction. They've enjoyed publishing on
Popular Woodworking's pages some of their favorite and
most useful Arts and Crafts designs. Some are replicas of
original pieces from the early 20th century, while others
are sensitive adaptations of existing designs.

Shaker projects are often mentioned as a great furniture style to facilitate learning woodworking. In our hum-
ble opinions, Arts and Crafts projects offer an excellent
"next step" in furthering a woodworker's education. Offering more complex joinery, a more varied range of project
types and a more challenging range of finishing choices,

Arts and Crafts furniture can hone a woodworker's skills,
while offering projects which can be successfully completed without years of training — and the pieces still offer a
simple, sturdy, classic appeal.

Many thanks go to photographer Al Parrish for cap-
turing the beauty of many of these projects. Also, a wel-
come to the Arts and Crafts fold goes out to Popular
Woodworking Books Editor Jim Stack; he tackled his first
Arts and Crafts project for this book. The Limbert Inlaid
Rocker is a beautiful piece that offers at least two more
skill-building opportunities: inlay and laminated bending.

Much of the beauty of Arts and Crafts furniture starts
with the wood, and so we'd like to thank the good folks at
Frank Miller Lumber Company of Union City, Indiana, for
allowing us to select some amazing quartersawn white oak
for our projects. We also want to express our appreciation
to Lee Valley Tools, Rockler Woodworking and Hardware,
and Van Dyke's Restorers for providing hardware that
helped us to put the finishing touches on our projects.

We hope you'll enjoy building the projects offered
here as much as we did. As long as the demand continues,
we'll be happy to keep offering Arts and Crafts projects in
Popular Woodworking.

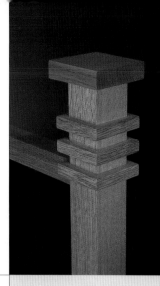

table of contents

by **Christopher Schwarz**

About Arts & Crafts Furniture

ARTS AND CRAFTS FURNITURE WAS THE PRODUCT of a brief but fruitful social movement in the United States at the turn of the 20th century. For a short moment in history, the American people declared they didn't want frilly, highly carved, machine-made stuff. They wanted furniture and decorative objects that were made by hand, with simple straight lines and honest construction. Furniture makers and philosophers gave the American people what they demanded (though sometimes they created it using machines) until consumers' attention turned to World War I. Though the Arts and Crafts period lasted less than 20 years, its societal and stylistic impact is still felt today by scholars, home decorators and woodworkers.

My first encounter with the Arts and Crafts movement occurred more than a decade ago in a foggy field outside Pickens, South Carolina. A friend and I had awoken before dawn that day to attend a farmers' market that promised fresh produce, Mennonite baked goods and the occasional piece of furniture pulled from a barn or an attic. As we left the truck, carrying flashlights and heading into the fog, we ran into four men toting shotguns. It was going to be a dangerous day ... but not because of the gun-wielding locals. I was facing the precipice of a deep hole from which few ever emerge: I was about to become a hard-core collector of all things Arts and Crafts.

The farmer's market was chock-full of men trading guns, military memorabilia, tools and other junk — which is the stuff we were looking for. One old guy had a truck that was almost completely covered in rust, except for the worn wooden gates on the sides that kept the stuff on his flatbed from spilling off the truck and onto the highway. This morning he had a few old dressers, some rusted metal things of unknown origin or use and one rocker.

The back of the rocker was covered by an uglyblanket and its runners were soaked with dew, but the minute I glimpsed the outline of the first Arts and Crafts piece I had ever seen, I was hooked. I learned later that the rocker was an old copy of a low-slung L.& J.G. Stickley piece, but all I knew back then was that it was only $30 and so it was going to be mine. I took it home, and my fiancée allowed it to occupy a corner of the office. A few weeks later, I bought a huge Arts and Crafts settee that concealed a massive iron bed frame. It was stuffed with the original horsehair and had been owned by the first African American doctor in Rome, Georgia. And it was only $125. So it, too, became mine.

For the next few years, I spent every spare dime of my disposable income on

Gustav Stickley.

"Great nations write their autobiographies in three manuscripts: the book of their words, the book of their deeds and the book of their art."

JOHN RUSKIN

Arts and Crafts furniture, books, pottery and metalwork. I went to lectures at the Grove Park Inn in Asheville, North Carolina. I spent hours poring over the reprints of manufacturers' catalogs that were just then becoming widely available. And I learned everything I could about how Arts and Crafts furniture was made: mortise and tenon, quadrilinear post construction, wedged and keyed through-tenons.

Of course, by 1993 it seemed the whole world was doing the same thing. And the newcomers had a lot more money. Soon, the pieces of furniture I wanted were selling at auction for prices that rivaled my yearly salary as a writer. Then, one day, I heard about a woodworking class at the University of Kentucky. The class focused on hand tools and traditional joints. At that moment, I knew I would become a woodworker.

The professor spent a lot of time teaching me and my classmates how to cut a mortise-and-tenon joint with a backsaw and a chisel. I cut mine as fast as I could in a piece of poplar. "Lynn," I asked, "could you show me how to cut a wedged through-tenon?" My instructor looked at me kind of funny. He built high-end modern stuff with lots of plywood and lots of bent laminations. "Why would you want to learn such an old-fashioned joint?" he asked. I didn't tell him why, because I certainly didn't need one more person interested in the Arts and Crafts movement. But he showed me how to do it with hand tools. Then he showed me how to use a hollow chisel mortiser, and I was hooked.

Too Expensive to Collect

For the average American, authentic Arts and Crafts furniture has become all but unaffordable. Furniture that is signed by its maker and has its original finish and upholstery now sells for thousands of dollars. Cabinetmakers sell authentic reproductions, but the good ones are, again, thousands of dollars. And the stuff available in furniture stores varies somewhere between not entirely bad and unspeakably awful. So,

Item #326, China cabinet, from a 1906 Shop of the Crafters at Cincinnati catalog.

it's official. The only way you are going to be able to afford authentic Arts and Crafts furniture is to build it yourself.

That's where this book comes in. During the last five years, David Thiel, Jim Stuard and I have been building Arts and Crafts furniture for our homes and for publication in *Popular Woodworking* magazine. Some of these designs have been adaptations. For example, the Arts and Crafts sideboard on page 94 owes a huge debt to four or

five sideboards produced by one or another of the Stickley brothers. But instead of creating a museum copy, David scaled the proportions down a bit to fit into a modern home. Other projects in this book have been taken from photos of original pieces, examples we found in museums or, in the case of the Shop of the Crafters Morris chair on page 22, an exact replica was made from the original.

Arts and Crafts furniture is remark-

ably simple to make. In fact, it's no coincidence that just as the Arts and Crafts movement was coming into its own in 1900, the manual training movement became an important force in schools. It was the first time American schools had sought to teach handicrafts, including woodworking and sewing. In fact, Gustav Stickley (1858–1942), one of the spiritual fathers of the movement, urged students in his shop class to build Arts and Crafts–style furniture because of its simple joinery and honest construction. So as you embark on building your own American classics, you can rest assured it has been part of the learning experience for woodworkers for more than a century.

The Mythical Movement

"In an age of debased design, the simplest style will be the best."
CHARLES LOCKE EASTLAKE

The Arts and Crafts movement itself was founded on good intentions, cloaked in philosophy and popularized through advertising and marketing. The now-popular legend is that the Arts and Crafts movement came about because people at the turn of the century rejected the mass-produced and ornate furnishings of the Victorian "Golden Oak" period and longed for furniture that was honest, simple and made by hand. And while it's true that the founders of the movement had pure intentions, the reality is that most of the people involved in producing Arts and Crafts goods during this period were more concerned with exploiting a furniture fad.

Most historians trace the origin of the American Arts and Crafts movement to Englishmen John Ruskin (1819–1900) and William Morris (1834–1896), whose name has been given to the Morris chair, though no one has ever been able to convince me he ever even sat in one. According to David M. Cathers' seminal work on the movement, *Furniture of the American Arts and Crafts Move-*

ment, Ruskin believed that the industrial age had dehumanized workers who were slaving in England's early industrial factories. To break the bonds of the machine and create an improved social order, workers needed to return to creating handmade objects. In essence, Ruskin wanted a return to the old medieval guild system.

William Morris agreed and came up with an idea to actually do something about the situation. He founded a company in 1861 that put these principles into practice. The idea was that people would make beautiful objects by hand that the middle class could afford. In this way, the workers' lives would be improved, and the level of taste and quality of goods in the marketplace would also improve. Unfortunately, as you probably well know, making things by hand is slow and very expensive. As it turned out, the only people who could afford Morris' beautiful wares were the very wealthy. So in 1881, Morris allowed machines into his workshop to remove the drudgery of routine tasks for his workers; it also made the furniture more affordable.

Morris' and Ruskin's ideas, however, were flourishing in the minds of the right people in America. Elbert Hubbard (1856–1915), the founder of the Roycrofters, and Gustav Stickley traveled to Europe and were exposed to these ideas. They came back to the United States and, within a year or two, a movement was born. Stickley spent some time experimenting with different designs and was producing his first line

Leopold Stickley.

of Craftsman furniture by 1900. Hubbard founded a printing company. After he expanded his building, he needed to give the carpenters something to do. Legend has it that they built a few tables for the new buildings. When visitors toured his place, they wanted to buy the tables, and so a new furniture company was born. Both companies were more like craftsmen's guilds than traditional cabinet shops of that time period. Both began producing furniture mostly by hand. And both would eventually reject this idea in order to stay in business.

As soon as other furniture makers saw the popularity of this new style, they began to copy it. They developed their own lines of furniture made from white oak, and they used the same marketing tactics employed by Stickley and Hubbard, who preached about the virtues of handmade furniture.

Charles P. Limbert's catalog No. 112 is a good example of some of the puffery that the public was eager to swallow. "Our heavy tops are solid

planks," Limbert wrote. "We use no strips on the edges to make them appear heavier." Well, I can tell you with certainty: That declaration is a load of bunk. I've inspected half of a dozen examples of his furniture that use build-up strips on the edges, as a matter of fact, one of them is in my living room. At the Roycroft Shop in East Aurora, New York, visitors were shown the work area, which featured some massive woodworking benches, a lot of hand tools and not a machine in sight. Visitors were never shown the mechanical tenon cutters, saws or sanders. Handmade objects were all the rage. But only the machine could deliver these products at a price the public could afford.

Most woodworkers, like myself, are quick to forgive the furniture makers of that time because we struggle with this same dilemma every day we're in the shop. I enjoy cutting dovetails by hand, but you'd have to pry my 8" biscuit jointer out of my cold, dead hands before I'd give it up. So is my work a product of handwork or is it merely machining the wood to an exact tolerance? Modern woodworking machines have reduced the tedium of many time-consuming tasks. Would you enjoy woodworking if you had to spend three solid days surfacing all your stock with a scrub plane? Probably not. So, if you feel a tinge of guilt as you fire up your hollow chisel mortiser, wondering if you're being true to the movement, you can rest assured that Stickley, Hubbard and others felt exactly the same way. And, in the end, they chose the path that took the drudgery out of construction and allowed the woodworker to enjoy the simple act of creation.

About the Manufacturers

Probably hundreds of companies were producing Arts and Crafts furniture around the turn of the century, and probably even more are producing it today. To give you a feel for the history behind the pieces in this book, we've included short profiles of the major manufacturers we've highlighted in this book, including the major stylistic elements you'd find on original pieces.

A Welsh cupboard similar to this drawing was noticed by Leopold Stickley during an exploratory visit to Chester, England.

Who Were the Brothers Stickley?

When most people see a piece of Arts and Crafts furniture, they inevitably ask if it's a Stickley. It's a horrible question to try to answer. That's because several Stickleys were building furniture at the time. Gustav Stickley had his own firm, Craftsman Workshop. His brothers, Leopold and John George, founded L. & J.G. Stickley. Brother Charles had his own firm called Stickley and Brandt. And all of the brothers were involved, at one time or another, with the Stickley Brothers company.

It's interesting to note that before the Arts and Crafts movement began about 1899, all five of the Stickley brothers were involved in building period reproduction chairs, exactly the kind of stuff that they would later rail against. The first brother to make this switch was, of course, Gustav. Between 1900 and 1916, Gustav's Craftsman Workshops in Eastwood, New York, produced what is now considered the best work of the day. His furniture is characterized by through-tenons that have been reinforced by dowels, bold but pleasing proportions and an absolutely first-class finish. Though most people think of Arts and Crafts furniture as universally dark brown, Gustav offered a finish that was brownish-green and another that had a tinge of gray. I've seen both of these finishes on original and reproduction furniture, and I'm sur-

prised more woodworkers haven't given them a try.

His case pieces are marked by heavy, copper hardware (though he is said to have preferred square oak knobs) and shiplapped backs that have a small chamfer on the seam between the boards. Later examples of his work show that he used a plywood back. All of his furniture was signed, usually with

Item #255 from an early-1900s Limbert catalog.

Popular Woodworking's reproduction of item #255, the Limbert Wastepaper Box. See the project on page 118.

an imprint of a joiner's compass and the Flemish expression, *Als ik kan*. This translates to *As I can*, or *As best I can*.

Gustav also published *The Craftsman* magazine — a publication devoted to all things Arts and Crafts. While it was a vehicle for selling his goods, *The Craftsman* also offered complete plans for furniture, a heavy dose of philosophy, as well as floor plans and decorating tips for the ideal home. By 1912, his business was in decline. The world went to war, and when that was over, there was little interest in the Arts and Crafts movement. The style had been supplanted by an interest in Art Deco styles originating in Europe, colonial pieces from America's past and, eventually, modernism that was inspired by machines. Gustav died in 1942 while living with his daughter. Apparently he was still experimenting with finishes to the very end; his descendants found small patches on the underside of the furniture in his room that had been used as sample boards.

L. & J.G. Stickley: The Other Brothers

Leopold and John George's company in Fayetteville, New York, is worthy of note because it survives to this day. The work that came from L. & J.G. Stickley looked a lot like the furniture from the Craftsman Workshop, with only minor alterations. According to Bruce Johnson's account of the company, L. & J.G. Stickley's copies were of the highest quality. Other imitators of Gustav's furniture would use dowels to assemble the furniture and simply nail a fake tenon end onto a leg to suggest a through-tenon. L. & J.G. Stickley's shop appeared dedicated to quality workmanship.

In fact, in a couple of instances, items produced by L. & J.G. Stickley exceeded the workmanship at Craftsman Workshop. For example, in order to get quartersawn ray flake on all four sides of a table leg, Gustav would glue quartersawn veneer onto the two sides that showed the plain-sawn grain. L. & J.G. Stickley used *quadrilinear post-construction*. This involves taking four

Item #340 from an early-1900s Limbert catalog.

Popular Woodworking's reproduction of item #340, the Limbert Two-Door Bookcase. See the project on page 60.

pieces of wood and essentially cutting a lock miter on all of the edges to make a table leg. It creates a superior leg.

Unlike their brother Gustav, Leopold and John George were willing to change their furniture line to match their customers' tastes. The company issued its last Arts and Crafts catalog in 1922 (six years after Gustav went out of business) and began producing a line of colonial reproduction furniture in cherry. The company's 1950 catalog is interesting because it reads exactly like the company's 1914 catalog. You only need to replace the word *oak* with the word *cherry:*

"It was furniture that took full advantage of the durability and workability of the wild cherry wood ... furniture with broad flat surfaces that revealed the beautiful figure of the wood to advantage and that melted into pools of liquid fire when candlelight gleamed onto its carefully rubbed and polished finish."

After Leopold's death in 1957, his descendants sold the business to Alfred and Aminy Audi, who began producing Arts and Crafts furniture again in 1989.

Other Stickleys

Furniture collectors generally consider the other companies bearing the Stickley name to have been manufacturers of lesser furniture, though occasionally one piece will surprise you. One of my favorite pieces of furniture is a Stickley and Brandt side chair with a spring seat. The workmanship and finish rivals that of pieces from the Craftsman Workshop.

Charles P. Limbert Company: Curves and Cutouts

Three of the projects in this book are reproductions from the Charles P. Limbert Company's catalog. Unlike many of the imitators of the day, Limbert's factory in Grand Rapids, Michigan, turned out an extensive line of Arts and Crafts furniture that was much less massive and rectilinear than the Stickley lines. Many of Limbert's pieces had a decidedly European influence. Curves and cutouts were common on some pieces. On other pieces, he clearly was trying to take customers away by imitating the Stickleys.

As customers' tastes changed, Limbert was ready. Late in the period he introduced a popular line of "Ebon-oak" furniture, which was made from oak inlaid with ebony. The rocking chair featured on page 36 is from this collection. It is considered one of the finest rockers of the era and commands a high price tag at auction.

Greene & Greene: Architects With a Flair for Furniture

It's not really fair to lump Charles and Henry Greene's architectural firm with furniture manufacturers, but it's necessary. The Greene brothers, like Frank Lloyd Wright, were not in the business of producing furniture. However, they wanted to design the furniture that went into the homes they built for wealthy clients. (And when the clients couldn't afford their furniture, they insisted the client purchase furniture from Gustav Stickley.)

Greene & Greene furniture is noteworthy because of its unabashed Asian influence. Instead of oak, Greene and Greene used mahogany as their primary wood. Instead of using straight stretchers on chairs or tables, the Greene brothers' furniture incorporated a "cloud lift," a gentle bump, into the designs. And their signature design element included placing inlaid ebony pegs into the major joints. Sometimes these pegs were structural; sometimes they concealed screws.

Like furniture designed by Wright, Greene & Greene designs are rare and highly sought after. Some pieces fetch hundreds of thousands of dollars. In fact, some pieces, such as the Greene & Greene entry bench featured on page 44 have disappeared altogether into the black market.

Limbert's Arts and Crafts workshop attached this leather tag trademark to each piece of cabinetwork they created.

Shop of the Crafters: European Designs for the Midwest Man

We've always had a soft spot in our hearts for furniture from the Shop of the Crafters because the company is located in the same town as our editorial offices: Cincinnati, Ohio. Oscar Onken (1858–1948) began as a picture framer and then in 1904 founded his own furniture company that produced a full line of Arts and Crafts furniture. The furniture was more European in flavor than most, and many pieces relied heavily on inlay or veneer. Unfortunately, the construction techniques Onken used were not always up to par with those used by the Stickleys. His Morris chairs, for example, used dowels at the major joints instead of mortise-and-tenon joints.

The Shop of the Crafters catalog was geared mostly toward men. The furniture itself was massive and overbuilt, sometimes to the point of looking clunky. And Onken's catalog was filled with cellarettes and smoking stands, two of the pieces of furniture reserved for a man's den of the period.

Roycroft Shop: Printing, Metalworking and Woodworking

Elbert Hubbard was a successful soap salesman who turned philosopher after an 1894 encounter with William Morris in England. Hubbard was impressed by Morris' press and his guild of workers who were making furniture, wallpaper, textiles and books. So Hubbard returned to the States and set up a company that imitated Morris' Kelmscott Press. From his shop in East Aurora, New York, Hubbard produced his magazine, *The Philistine*, and a series of books called *Little Journeys*, which contained biographies of influential reformers (including Morris), philosophers, musicians and scientists.

His campus and his flamboyant personality attracted the attention of the public, which flocked to his shop. They wanted to buy the furniture they saw there, and he let them. According to Bruce Johnson, it's unlikely that Hubbard designed the furniture made by the Roycroft Shop; that task was handled by others. But the furniture is some of the most massive and well built on the antique market today. And it was considerably more expensive than furniture sold by Gustav Stickley. Even as the demand for the heavy furniture waned and other manufacturers began to shift gears, the Roycrofters stuck to their guns, even after Hubbard himself was drowned in the sinking of the *Lusitania* in 1915. Furniture making continued until the 1930s, but by 1938 the shop was bankrupt.

Byrdcliffe Arts Colony: Perhaps Earliest Hippies in Woodstock

The Byrdcliffe Arts Colony was an experimental utopian community founded by Ralph Radcliffe Whitehead (1854–1929) in 1902 in Woodstock,

New York. It was to be a place where artists and craftsmen could work together to produce beautiful objects for sale much like a modern-day commune.

It never quite worked out that way. Wendy Kaplan estimates the colony turned out fewer than 50 pieces of furniture. Apparently some of the pieces were so heavy and massive that shipping them was difficult. And because they were made by hand — frequently with carvings — they were unaffordable for most people. By 1905, the founder — Ralph Radcliffe Whitehead — had closed the woodshop.

Isn't Arts and Crafts Just Another Furniture Fad?

In 1990, a friend of mine who had been collecting Arts and Crafts furniture for five years told me that I should wait to purchase a few antique pieces because the bottom of the market was about to fall out. According to him, the Arts and Crafts revival, which had begun in the 1970s, was going to take a serious nose-dive, and soon the furniture would be affordable for everyone. At the time, I was eyeing a Shop of the Crafters Morris chair that had been languishing in an Anderson, South Carolina, antiques market for months with a $360 price tag.

"Just wait," he said. "And the price will come down."

I couldn't wait. I bought the chair. And it's lucky I did. The bottom has yet to fall out of the market. The American public has a seemingly inexhaustible hunger for all things Arts and Crafts — from Morris chairs to the plates that cover your light switches. The current revival, according to some estimates, has now lasted longer than the original movement. But, every year, I hear the same refrain from people inside and out of the movement: It's going to end some day, so watch out. Perhaps they're afraid they'll end up like Gustav Stickley did, forgotten and living with his daughter, experimenting with finishes on tiny patches of wood on the underside of his bedroom furniture.

Now, I'm sure that the craze surrounding Arts and Crafts will die down a bit. And maybe some of the people

William Morris.

who are producing junk won't be able to sell it anymore. But the important thing to remember here is that the Arts and Crafts style has now been recognized as an important period in furniture history, like the heyday of 18th-century American cabinetmaking. And while colonial reproductions are hard to come by in the superstores, the market for authentic antiques and quality handmade reproductions in this style is as strong as ever. This is likely the future of Arts and Crafts.

So if you enjoy the clean lines and honest workmanship of Arts and Crafts furniture, I think you are going to enjoy this book and relish the furniture you build using it. And if you take extra special care to peg all of your tenons with dowels, if you account for wood movement as best you can, and if you cut each joint as tight as possible, I'm sure your great-grandchildren are going to feel the same way about your furniture, too.

by Christopher Schwarz and David Thiel

Construction and Finishing Techniques

EACH OF THE PROJECT CHAPTERS IN THIS BOOK includes step-by-step construction directions that should provide adequate information for all but the very new woodworker to successfully build each project. We've also included the specific finishing processes used for each individual project. We'll talk more about finishing later. Where possible we have endeavored to teach new methods and simplify complicated processes.

In addition to these fairly thorough directions, we felt it appropriate to include this section on construction and finishing techniques of specific use in Arts and Crafts furniture designs. While none of these joints or finishing techniques is unique to Arts and Crafts furniture (except for ammonia fuming for finishing), when a number of them occur in a single piece there's a good chance it fits in the Arts and Crafts category.

Construction

In the next pages we will discuss construction techniques for a number of types of mortise-and-tenon joints, including blind, through, pegged, wedged and keyed tenons. We will also take a look at the use of quadrilinear construction for legs and posts, corbels for esthetics and support, shiplapped construction for use with solid wood backs, and the use of pattern routing to make identical esthetic shapes. With basic woodworking knowledge and the detailed instruction of these techniques,

you will be able to build almost any Arts and Crafts furniture piece.

Mortise and Tenon

It's not really going too far to say that you can't build a piece of Arts and Crafts furniture without using a mortise-and-tenon joint somewhere. The type and complexity of mortise-and-tenon joint varies from project to project, but this was a really popular joint with the Arts and Crafts craftsman. Happily, they weren't nearly as fond of dovetails, which take a bit more skill.

The basic mortise-and-tenon joint, or blind tenon, consists of a square hole cut into one piece of wood, with a correspondingly sized nub cut on the end of the mating piece of wood. Square peg A in square hole B. Simple. This joint gets used in chair construction to join legs and stretchers, to attach back splats to back rails and then the back rails to the back legs. Simple mortise-and-tenon joinery also sees frequent use in stile-and-rail door construction and in stile-and-rail panel construction in case pieces. And this makes lots of sense because the strength offered from this joint is amazing. When you add the option of wedged or pegged tenons the joint is nearly indestructible. Make it a through-tenon with a key, and this remarkably strong joint can be easily taken apart to collapse the piece of furniture and move it easily. The mortise and tenon are handy and versatile

joints, so let's talk about how to make them.

There are two basic schools of thought on all mortise-and-tenon construction. In one, you cut the mortise, or hole, first, then fit the tenon to the mortise. In the other, you make the tenon first and then fit the mortise. Neither is wrong, but the mortise-first method has benefits that most of us at Popular Woodworking agree with. So let's start with making the mortise, and hopefully you'll see why it's the better method.

Mortises

There are a few ways to make a mortise. The traditional method is with a chisel and mallet, defining the shape of the mortise and slowly paring away the wood with the chisel. If you count the number of mortises in either the box spindle chair project or the sideboard project, you may decide hand cutting isn't a very labor-conscious method. The tool of choice is a dedicated square-chisel mortiser. Designed to cut ¼", ⅜" or ½" mortises, these clever tools not only drill out the hole, but with the use of an attached four-sided chisel, they square the corners. The mortiser allows you to set the depth of the mortise, and make accurate, square mortises, quickly and with relatively little difficulty. While you may not be looking for more machinery for your shop, if you plan on building any amount of Arts and Crafts furniture, you may want to seriously consider a mortiser.

Another option is to use an existing drill press. While the drill press won't square out the corners of the mortise for you, it certainly will speed up the operation. Then you head back to basics and simply square out the corners with your hand chisel. Another option with a drill press is a mortising attachment. This attachment pretty much turns your drill press into a mortiser. The one difference is the distance the drill press lever must travel to create the same depth hole as the mortiser. Because of the way the machines are geared, the mortiser can create the same hole with a third of the travel necessary on a drill press.

No matter which method you choose, the mortising process is the same. Start by carefully marking the location of the mortise. The usual procedure is to cut the mortise in the center of the face of the piece. The mortise width should be one-third the thickness of the piece, and the depth should be approximately two-thirds the width. So if your door stile is ¾" × 1½", the mortise should be ⅜" wide, centered on the ¾" face, and be approximately 1" deep. The mortise formed by this method is referred to as a blind mortise and tenon because the joinery will not be visible on the finished piece.

The only other option is a through-mortise, which is cut all the way through the piece of wood. In any through-cutting situation, take care to avoid tear-out on the "exit" side of the mortise. The easiest way to do this is by using a backing piece. While this piece will help a lot, there will probably be some tear-out. Make sure that the tear-out side is on the face that the tenon's shoulder will seat against, helping to hide the imperfect mortise.

Tenons

Now that we've talked about mortises, let's look at the tenons. A tenon can be cut a few different ways. Either two or four sides can be pared away (basically performing a rabbet cut), to leave less than the thickness or width of the piece. The sides of the tenons are re-

Mortiser in use.

Cutting a tenon on a table saw.

ferred to as the cheeks, and the top of the notch left after the cut is referred to as the shoulder. If a tenon is cut with four cheeks, the shoulders will hide imperfections caused by cutting the mortise. Since the usual shoulder is only about ³⁄₁₆" wide, it won't hide everything, but if your mortise is that sloppy, it won't make a very good joint either.

To cut a tenon, the most usual method is to use a table saw. A router table can also be used, and there's still the old faithful handsaw if you've got the extra time and energy. To make tenons on the table saw, the first step is to define the shoulder, thereby determining the length of the tenon. Set your rip fence for the length of the tenon, including the blade thickness in the dimension (you'll be cutting the shoulder height to the left of the blade). You should cut the tenon ¹⁄₁₆" shorter than the depth of your mortise to leave a

place for the glue to pool. Square the miter gauge to the blade, and with the blade set at a height to cut a little less than the shoulder width, lay the tenon piece flat on the saw; with the end against the rip fence, push the miter gauge and piece through the blade, cutting on two or four sides as required. For example, if you are cutting a tenon for the above-mentioned ⅜"-wide, by 1"-deep mortise on ¾" material, the rip fence is likely set for ¹³⁄₁₆" (including the ⅛" blade thickness), and the blade height would be set for a little less than ³⁄₁₆" high. All four sides can be cut with this setting.

Next, reset the fence for the width of the tenon, plus the width of the shoulder, and change the height of the blade to the actual length of the tenon. In our example this would be ¹⁄₁₆" between the fence and blade, and the height would be ¹⁵⁄₁₆". By running the piece on end with the wider side against the fence, the two wider cheeks are formed. The fence is then reset to trim the two other cheeks to size. Some woodworkers choose to cut the cheeks first, then define the shoulders, but by following that order you will end up with the waste piece trapped between the blade and fence, causing a kickback.

Unless you have a certain amount of comfort and experience on the table saw, running the cheek cuts with the piece upright is best performed with a support jig behind the piece to keep the piece square to the table and to help control the cut. Another option is a tenoning jig designed for the table saw to cut tenons. While a useful, accurate and efficient device, it costs a little more, and I actually find it a little time-consuming. Still another option, and also time-consuming, is to leave the piece lying flat after the initial shoulder-defining cut and use repeat passes to nibble away the rest of the tenon waste.

Although following these steps to cut the tenon should give you an accurate fit to your mortise, you should cut test pieces to check the size as you go. A mortise-and-tenon joint should be a snug fit, but you shouldn't have to use too much force to put it together. Also, too loose and your joint will have less strength. It's best to have the tenons a little thicker than necessary, then carefully fit them to the mortise with a shoulder plane, chisel or a little sanding.

Through-Tenons

Beyond the basic blind mortise and tenon is the through-tenon. With the mortise cut all the way through the piece, either the tenon can be cut flush, then wedged into the end of the tenon, or it can be left long to extend beyond the outer face of the piece. If left long, the end of the tenon can be chamfered on four edges to leave a decorative edge, then pegged (we'll talk more about this in a minute). Or the tenon can be left very long and a key added to secure the joint (more about this, as well).

Pegged Tenons

Pegging a tenon is a great way to make an already strong joint even stronger. To peg a tenon, after it has been glued and seated in place in the mortise, drill a hole through the side of the leg or other mortised piece, going through the center of the tenon and on through into the opposite side of the mortise. Insert a dowel of corresponding diameter to the hole and glue it in place in the hole, then cut the dowel flush to the surface. The extra strength provided by this "wooden nail" should be obvious at this point, but over time it will be even more useful. As wood ages, it has a tendency to shrink a little, which can allow a tight mortise-and-tenon joint to loosen up.

The peg can hold the joint tight, even if the tenon shrinks in the mortise. Pegging is a fine idea for blind or through-tenon construction.

Keyed Tenons

In a keyed tenon, another through-mortise is drilled in the extended length of the tenon (partially hidden by the mortised leg or piece), and another piece of wood (the key), cut in the shape of a wedge, is tapped into the hole to pull the joint tight. The keys can be plain or decorative depending on the designer or your choice. Specific directions for through-tenon, pegged and keyed joints are included with the individual projects.

Through-mortise and wedged tenon.

Quadrilinear post.

Corbel shown at junction of front leg and arm of chair.

Quadrilinear Posts

One of the most appealing features in the somewhat understated Arts and Crafts furniture is the beauty of the wood figure. Use traditional quarter-sawn white oak in a piece and two faces of each piece will show the attractive medullary rays, which appear as flakes or bands of lighter translucent material. To use this figure to its best design capability, it would be great to have the rays show on every face. This isn't really possible on all pieces, but it can, and has been, achieved on legs and posts. While Gustav Stickley opted to add quarter-sawn veneer to the non-quarter-sawn faces, his brother Leopold came up with a mechanical (and more durable) method he dubbed the quadrilinear post. If you take thinner (¾") material and miter the long edges, the glued-up post will have four quarter-sawn faces. Add a strip in the center of the hollow piece to form a solid post. Not only is this attractive, but this is also a more economical use of materials. Leopold went even further than just mitering the edge and formed an interlocking miter. A variation on that locking miter is now available as a router bit used in box building to form a lock-miter joint. While it works great for boxes, Leopold

would recognize its benefit on the quadrilinear post. Setup for using the lock-miter bit takes some precision, but once the bit is set up in a router table, the final visual effect is dramatic.

Corbels

A fairly distinctive feature in Arts and Crafts furniture is the use of sweeping bracketlike supports to stabilize tops, arms and seats. These supports, or corbels, offer a delicate style element as well as strengthening the piece. Though the corbel is not peculiar to Arts and Crafts furniture (the shape and use is found in a number of architectural designs), it is common to the style. Corbels are seen in a number of shapes and sizes, and while we've provided some instruction on how they should look in the specific projects, we recommend a certain amount of personal choice to help make the piece your own. Corbels are simple to make once the shaped is determined. After rough-cutting the pieces to shape on the band saw, clamp the pieces together (corbels hardly ever travel alone), and sand them smooth and to match. Attaching corbels is simple. Because of the grain orientation, corbels can be glued to a leg or cabinet side with simple clamping pressure, forming a strong long-grain glue joint.

Shiplapped Boards

An awful lot of today's cabinetry uses ¼"-thick plywood for backs. Our ancestors didn't have that commercial luxury and instead used solid wood backs. But one-piece solid wood backs are an unstable construction detail and definitely not economical. So they borrowed a joint from their shipbuilding brethren and used an overlapping edge joint, allowing them to use solid boards of random and thinner width to form the back. Frequently they added a slight chamfer to the joined edges of the boards to further separate the pieces. This design appears in many Arts and Crafts pieces, and while some of the projects in this book have substituted plywood backs for economic reasons, the shiplap design is an authentic and attractive design element.

Pattern Routing

Another frequent design element is the use of arches on stretchers and aprons. Even more prevalent in the work of the Greene & Greene brothers is the use of stepped designs on the stretchers and aprons with rounded corners. The Greene brothers referred to this design element as a cloud lift, and the design has decidedly Asian influences. In most cases these design elements repeat

Shiplapped backs.

Cloud lift pattern routing.

identically on pieces. To get them to match, pattern routing is a handy technique. Make a plywood template in the shape of the required piece, then use a router bit with a ball-bearing guide to make any number of pieces in the same shape. This process is valuable in many of the projects in this book.

Finishing Arts and Crafts Furniture

Achieving the perfect finish on a piece of Arts and Crafts furniture is perhaps the biggest challenge faced when building in this style. After all, the designs are generally straightforward and the construction techniques are not difficult to master with a little practice. We've tried dozens of different ways to color the wood to achieve that perfect, mellow tone so indicative of Arts and

Crafts. And while we haven't found the perfect one-step solution, we're a lot closer than we were five years ago.

Sanding

Before you color your wood, pay attention to the sanding process. White oak is a tough wood that requires more sanding than other cabinet woods such as cherry or maple. For sanding white oak, we recommend using a random orbit sander. Begin at 100-grit, then go to 120 and, finally, 150. Now, stop. Here's the thing: random orbit sanders minimize the scratches left on the wood, but with white oak, you need to go one step further. If you want to eliminate the tiny "pig tails" or swirls that soak up stain, you have to hand sand your project.

Use a sanding block loaded with 150-grit paper, turn on the radio and turn off your brain. This is the only road we know to a swirl-free finish. As you sand, examine the surface with a low, raking light source, such as one of those job-site lights you can buy at home-center stores for about $20. It will clarify any swirls left on the surface and let you know when it's time to stop sanding.

Ammonia Fuming

Gustav Stickley and his imitators fumed their oak furniture with ammonia. This is the one method for coloring wood we haven't tried. Stickley recommended in an issue of *The Craftsman* magazine that the home woodworker fume furniture in this manner: The furniture must be fumed in an airtight room. One solution is to build a fuming tent from sheets of plastic and 2×4s. Or if you have to fume an entire roomful of furniture at once, there's the story about a guy who rented a van from U-Haul or Ryder and fumed all the pieces in there.

Once the furniture is in an airtight room, place shallow dishes of high-strength ammonia in the room, seal it up and wait. Ammonia purchased at the neighborhood grocery store isn't strong enough; find someone who sells aqua ammonia (a mixture containing 26 percent ammonia). Stickley said 48

Arts and Crafts finishes can be tough to get "just right." After five years of practice, we've come up with a method that pleases us. This Stickley side table was finished with a water-based dye, followed by a coat of boiled linseed oil, a coat of glaze, then three coats of a clear finish.

hours should be a long enough time period to produce the desired color. The longer you wait, the darker the color. After 48 hours, lightly sandpaper the surfaces, then fume the piece again. Then add a top coat of wax, shellac or another clear finish.

Is ammonia the best way to finish Arts and Crafts furniture? According to some people who have done it, the jury is still out. Stickley himself said the process can be troublesome. Two different wood types may change color in different ways, especially if one contains more tannic acid than the other. This can be a real nightmare for a beginning finisher. Other woodworkers, however, have reported success with this method.

It's also a good idea to keep in mind that fuming a piece of furniture with ammonia can be dangerous. The fumes can knock you out if you're not careful. Unless you know what you are doing or are working with someone who does, we recommend you stick to traditional stains, dyes and glazes.

Dye and Glaze

Some of the nicest finishes we've achieved incorporated a reddish water-based dye, followed by a coat of shellac, then a coat of warm brown glaze, followed by three coats of a clear finish. If using a water-based dye, rag a thin coat of clear water over the entire project before you apply the dye. Water, as you know, raises the grain of the wood. Allow the water to dry, then sand off the raised grain by hand with 150-grit sandpaper. Now, when the dye is applied, it won't raise the grain nearly as much.

Our reddish dye of choice is Moser's Light Sheraton Mahogany, available from Woodworkers Supply, (800) 645-9292. It comes in a powder that is to be mixed with hot water. Follow the directions on the package, then dilute it by half. Rag it on your project using a lint-free cloth. Be careful not to overlap the edges too much; the color can build up quickly. Allow the dye to dry overnight.

Moser also makes an alcohol-based version of this dye, but it is more susceptible to fading than the water-based. However, it does dry faster.

Next, seal the wood to prepare for glazing. This can be done any number of ways: Add a coat of boiled linseed oil and let it dry overnight; or brush/wipe on a thin coat of orange shellac or wiping varnish (varnish that has been thinned with mineral spirits). Shellac gives a warmer tone than a clear finish does and dries much faster than a wiping varnish does. Once this sealing coat is dry, don't worry that it looks so red. Adding the warm brown glaze will "kill" some of the red color.

Most woodworkers are mystified by

Always make a sample board of your work before you color your project. That way, you won't have to learn about "refinishing" just yet.

glaze. Essentially, it's a thin paint or a thick stain professional painters use for faux effects. It always goes on between coats of a film finish. If applied directly to the wood, it's not glazing, it's staining. Sometimes that works fine, too, though you should try a sample board using only glaze and a top coat. We use a glaze made by Lilly Industries that, as far as we know, isn't available through mail order. Check your local professional paint store. It costs us about $26 a gallon.

Applying glaze is easy. Use a cheesecloth to apply a thin coat to one surface of your project. Let the glaze set up for a few minutes and allow it to "flash." This means that the surface of the finish goes from shiny to dull. Then, take a second cheesecloth and begin wiping away the excess glaze with even and gentle strokes. Wipe the surface until you achieve the tone you want and then stop. Now, move on to the next surface.

When your entire project is glazed, allow it to sit overnight. Cover it with three coats of a clear finish, sanding between coats with a 3M sanding sponge (fine grit) or 360-grit lubed sandpaper.

Other Options

We've tried the Instant Age finish with some success. On its own, the color is a bit anemic. Once we added a coat of a cherry gel stain, it was perfect. Of course, that process takes as long as the dye-and-glaze method and is a bit more expensive. To color your project green, try an aniline dye. Moser makes a Dark Forest Green shade that looks just right for Arts and Crafts furniture. Follow it with a coat of glaze to produce a color that looks like the finish on one of the tables at Stickley's Craftsman Farms.

If you are interested in a lighter finish, you can try another process recommended by Stickley. Cover your project with boiled linseed oil and set your project out in the full sun for an afternoon. Add another coat of oil and repeat this process until you get a mellow and aged (but significantly lighter) finish. Follow all this with a protective top coat.

Common Stains and Topcoats

STAINS

STAIN TYPE	FORM	PREPARATION	CHARACTERISTICS
Pigment stains			
Oil-based	Liquid	Mix thoroughly	Apply with rag, brush or spray; resists fading.
Water-based	Liquid	Mix thoroughly	Apply with rag, brush or spray; resists fading; water cleanup.
Gel	Gel	Ready to use	Apply with rag; won't raise grain; easy to use; no drips or runs.
Water-based gel	Gel	Ready to use	Apply with rag; easy to use; no drips or runs.
Japan color	Concentrated liquid	Mix thoroughly	Used for tinting stains, paints, varnish, lacquer.
Dye stains			
Water-based	Powder	Mix with water	Apply with rag, brush or spray; deep penetrating; best resistance of dye stains; good clarity; raises grain.
Oil-based	Powder	Mix with toluol, lacquer thinner, turpentine or naphtha	Apply with rag, brush or spray; penetrating; does not raise grain; dries slowly.
Alcohol-based	Powder	Mix with alcohol	Apply with rag, brush or spray; penetrating; does not raise grain; dries quickly, lap marks sometimes a problem.
NGR	Liquid	Mix thoroughly	Apply with rag, brush or spray (use retarder if wiping or brushing); good clarity; does not raise grain.

TOPCOATS

FINISH TYPE	FORM	PREPARATION	CHARACTERISTICS	DRY TIME
Shellac	Liquid	Mix thoroughly	Dries quickly; economical; available either clear or amber-colored; high gloss luster; affected by water, alcohol and heat.	2 hours
Shellac flakes	Dry flakes	Mix with alcohol	Dries quickly; economical (mix only what is needed); color choices from amber to clear; high gloss luster; affected by water, alcohol and heat.	2 hours
Lacquer	Liquid	Mix with thinner for spraying	Dries quickly; clear (shaded lacquers available); high gloss luster, but flattening agents available; durable; moisture resistant.	30 minutes
Varnish	Liquid	Mix thoroughly	Dries slowly; amber color; gloss, semi-gloss and satin lusters; very good durability and moisture resistance; flexible.	3 to 6 hours
Polyurethane	Liquid	Mix thoroughly	Dries slowly; clear to amber colors; gloss, semi-gloss and satin lusters; excellent durability and moisture resistance; flexible.	3 to 6 hours
Water-based polyurethane	Liquid	Mix thoroughly	Dries quickly; clear; won't yellow; gloss and satin lusters; moisture and alcohol resistant; low odor.	2 hours
Tung oil	Liquid	Ready to use	Dries slowly; amber color; satin luster; poor moisture resistance; easy to use.	20 to 24 hours
Danish oil	Liquid	Mix thoroughly	Dries slowly; amber color; satin luster; poor moisture resistance; easy to use.	8 to 10 hours

NOTE: Dry times are based on a temperature of 70° Fahrenheit and 40-percent relative humidity. Lower temperature and/or higher relative humidity can increase drying time.

Almost every woodworker has the skills to build
the most comfortable chair in the house.

Morris Chair

I DON'T CARE WHAT THEY SAY ABOUT
DOGS, Morris chairs are a man's best
friend. The reclining back, wide arms
and expansive seat create the perfect
place to watch TV, read the Sunday
paper or simply contemplate the finer
qualities of a well-crafted beer.

For the last 10 years, I've spent every
weekend planted in the original version
of this chair, which was built by the
Shop of the Crafters in Cincinnati, Ohio,
during the heyday of the Arts and Crafts
movement. The Shop of the Crafters
was founded by German-American busi-
nessman Oscar Onken (1858–1948),
who ran a successful framing company
until he entered the furniture business
in 1902, according to Kenneth R.
Trapp's history of the company.

Unlike many furniture makers of the
day, Onken didn't want to merely copy
the Stickleys of the world. Onken produced an unusual line of Arts and
Crafts furniture that was influenced
more by German and Hungarian designs
than by the straight-lined Stickley
pieces of the day. In all honesty, a few
of Onken's pieces were kind of ugly.
Most, however, had a refinement and
lightness that rivaled some of the best
work of the day.

This Morris chair is an almost exact
replica of the one produced by Onken
and his company. It differs in only two
ways. One, the original chair was con-
structed using dowels at the major
joints. After almost 100 years of use,
the front and back rail came loose. This
chair is built using pegged mortise-and-
tenon joints. Second, I made one
change to the chair frame so that furniture historians of the future will know
instantly that this not an original piece.
I did this to prevent people from pass-
ing off these reproductions as originals.

Though this project might look
daunting to you, it can be completed by
beginners who have just a few projects
under their belts. There are only a few
principles to learn here: mortising,
tenoning, and routing with a plywood
template. Plus, I'll share with you exactly how I achieved this finish, which
is one we've been working on for several years.

How to Save Money on Lumber

Begin by choosing the right quarter-
sawn white oak for this project. It requires about 10 board feet of 8/4 and
30 board feet of 4/4 lumber. Quartered
white oak can be expensive, from $6 to
$12 a board foot. If you live in the Mid-
west, or will pass near east-central Indiana on your vacation, I recommend you
check out Frank Miller Lumber Company in Union City, Indiana, (800) 345-
2643, www.frankmiller.com. The
company is a huge supplier of quarter-
sawn oak. As a result, prices are reason-
able, about $4 to $6 a board foot. Once
you buy your lumber, save the pieces
with the most ray flake for the arms,
legs, front and sides. To save money,
use flat-sawn oak for the seat and the
adjustable back.

SUPPLIES

Slotted Piano Hinge
Rockler Woodworking
and Hardware:
(800) 279-4441 or
www.rockler.com
Item # 19241 • $6.99

Moser's Aniline Dye
Woodworker's Supply:
(800) 645-9292
Medium red mahogany,
alcohol soluble
Item # A16701 • $8.80

Warm Brown Glaze
Made by Lilly Industries
(formerly Guardsman).
For a list of distributors
of Lilly wood products,
visit the company's Web
site at: http://www.lillyin-
dustries.com

Climb-Cutting Tenons

I own a commercial tenoning jig for my table saw, but I rarely use it. I get better and faster results cutting tenons using a dado stack and a trick contributing editor Troy Sexton showed me. To avoid tear-out on my tenons' shoulders, I "climb-cut" the last $1/8$" or so of the tenon shoulder. You may have heard of climb-cutting using a router; it means moving the router the opposite way you normally would to avoid tear-out in tricky grain. That's exactly what you do on your table saw. The final cut on your shoulders is made by pulling the work toward you over the blade, taking only a small cut of material. It sounds awkward, but after a few tenons, you get used to it. The risk of kickback is minimal;

there's no wood trapped between the blade and the fence. To do this safely, hold your work steady. Here's how you do it: Install a dado stack into your table saw and set the fence for the finished length of your tenon (almost all of the tenons in this project are $3/4$" long). Set the height of your dado stack to the amount you want to thin one side of your tenon (for most of the tenons in this project, that's $3/16$"). Using your miter gauge, push the work through the dado stack to cut the majority of the tenon. Then slide the work against the fence and pull the miter gauge back toward you to shave the shoulder of the tenon. Flip the work over and do the other side. Then do the edges.

Make the mortises in the legs before you shape the curve near the bottom or make cutouts on the top.

Set your fence so the dado stack will make a $3/4$" cut (the length of your tenon). Hold the piece about $1/8$" from the fence. Push your work through the blade using your miter gauge.

After you finish that first pass, slide the work against the fence and pull it back toward you over the blade to shave the last little bit of the shoulder.

Repeat the same procedure for the edges of the tenon. (If you like a little more shoulder on your edges, increase the height of the blade.) First push the work forward.

Then slide it against the fence and pull it back toward you to make the final shoulder cut.

When pattern-routing the curve on the legs, make sure you have the work firmly clamped in place. I have the pattern and leg wedged between two pieces of oak (the pattern is on the underside of the leg). Then the leg itself is clamped to the table. You also could perform this operation on a router table with a starting pin for pattern-routing.

Mortises: Machine or No Machine?

First, cut all your pieces to size according to the Schedule of Materials and begin laying out the locations of your mortises. The rule of thumb is that your mortises should be one-half the thickness of your tenon's stock. When your

stock is $3/4$" thick, your mortises and tenons should be $3/8$" thick. That means the tenons for the beefy back rail should be thicker ($7/16$"), and those for the side slats should be thinner ($1/4$").

Also remember that except for the tenons on the legs and slats, all the tenons are $3/4$" long. To ensure your

tenons don't bottom out in your mortises, it's always a good idea to make your mortises about $1/16$" deeper than your tenons are long.

After you mark the locations of all the mortises, it's time to cut them. There are 38 mortises in this project. You'd be nuts to do these all by hand. Use this project as an excuse to purchase a hollow chisel mortising machine (about $250) or a mortising attachment for your drill press (about $70). If you can't swing the cash, I'd make plywood templates and cut the mortises with a router and a pattern bit. Making plywood templates is covered later in the chapter.

One more thing: Don't cut the mortises in the arms or the arm buildups until the chair frame is assembled. Cut these with a router and a pattern bit after the chair frame is assembled.

Schedule of Materials: Morris Chair

CHAIR FRAME

No.	Item	Dimensions T W L	Comments
2	Front legs	$1^{5}/_{8}" \times 3^{3}/_{4}" \times 21"$	$^{1}/_{2}"$ TOE
2	Back legs	$1^{5}/_{8}" \times 2^{1}/_{4}" \times 21"$	$^{1}/_{2}"$ TOE
2	Applied sides	$1^{5}/_{8}" \times 1^{3}/_{16}" \times 4"$	
1	Front rail	$^{3}/_{4}" \times 4^{3}/_{4}" \times 22"$	$^{3}/_{4}"$ TOE
2	Side rails	$^{3}/_{4}" \times 4^{3}/_{4}" \times 24"$	$^{3}/_{4}"$ TBE
1	Back rail	$^{7}/_{8}" \times 4^{3}/_{4}" \times 22"$	$^{3}/_{4}"$ TBE
2	Side slats	$^{1}/_{2}" \times 7^{5}/_{8}" \times 11^{3}/_{8}"$	$^{1}/_{2}"$ TBE
2	Arm blups.	$^{7}/_{8}" \times 6" \times 4^{1}/_{2}"$	
2	Arms	$^{3}/_{4}" \times 6" \times 35^{1}/_{4}"$	
2	Cleats	$^{3}/_{4}" \times 1^{7}/_{8}" \times 20^{1}/_{2}"$	
1	Back rod	$^{3}/_{4}" \times 2" \times 23^{5}/_{16}"$	

DROP-IN SEAT

No.	Item	Dimensions T W L	Comments
2	Seat stiles	$^{3}/_{4}" \times 2^{1}/_{2}" \times 23^{1}/_{2}"$	
5	Seat rails	$^{3}/_{4}" \times 2^{1}/_{2}" \times 17"$	$^{3}/_{4}"$ TBE

ADJUSTABLE BACK

No.	Item	Dimensions T W L	Comments
2	Back stiles	$^{3}/_{4}" \times 1^{7}/_{8}" \times 28^{1}/_{4}"$	
5	Back rails	$^{3}/_{4}" \times 1^{7}/_{8}" \times 17^{1}/_{2}"$	$^{3}/_{4}"$ TBE
1	Bot. rail	$^{3}/_{4}" \times 3^{1}/_{4}" \times 17^{1}/_{2}"$	$^{3}/_{4}"$ TBE

TOE = tenon on one end • TBE = tenon on both ends

Tenons With a Dado Stack

Once you get your mortises cut, make tenons that fit snugly into the mortises. You can use a tenoning jig or the fence on your table saw, or you can use a router. I prefer to use a dado stack and my miter gauge. See "Climb-Cutting Tenons" for details on how to do this.

While your dado stack is in your saw, cut the groove in the back piece that holds the seat frame. See the drawing for the location of this groove.

Once you cut your tenons, prepare to assemble the drop-in seat and the adjustable back. To save yourself some grief, sand the edges of the rails that you won't be able to get to after the frames are assembled. Now put glue in all the mortises and clamp up the frames. Set them aside to dry.

Curves and Cutouts

What makes this Morris chair stand out are the curves and cutouts on the legs, arms and slats. Each curve and cutout needs a slightly different strategy.

I cut the large curves on the legs and the small curves on the side slats using a plywood template and a pattern-cutting bit in a router. I made the patterns from $^{1}/_{2}"$-thick Baltic birch plywood. Use the drawings to make your own plywood template using a scroll saw, band

To make a template for the mortises in the arms and the cutouts on the side slats, position your plywood over your table saw and raise the blade into the ply. Move the fence over and repeat. Then turn the pattern 90 degrees and repeat for the other edges of the pattern. Note that I made cuts in the front of the pattern to help me size the pattern to the tenons.

saw or coping saw. Smooth all your cuts with sandpaper, then try shaping a couple scraps with your template to make sure your pattern produces the right shape. When satisfied, cut the curves to rough shape on your band saw (about $^{1}/_{16}"$ shy of your finished line) and clean up the cut with a router and pattern bit. Finish shaping the legs with a chisel.

To produce the large cutouts on the front legs, do what Oscar Onken did:

The "X" on the rails and cleats shoulder a frame nor her rather than an end view.

Peg the tenons that join the front rail to the front legs and the back rail to the back legs. If you've ever pegged tenons before, you know that dowels can be wildly different sizes than they're supposed to be. Here's a trick: If your dowel is a bit undersized, glue it in place and cut it nearly flush to the surface. Then put several drops of thinned glue on the end grain of the dowel. It wicks in the glue, expands and glues up tight. When the glue is dry, cut the dowel flush.

cheat a bit. Make the "cutouts" using a dado stack on your table saw, with the legs on edge. Then glue the applied sides to the legs to cover the open end of the cuts. Instant cutout. While you're at it, cut out the notches on the arm pieces for the rod that adjusts the back.

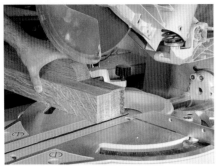

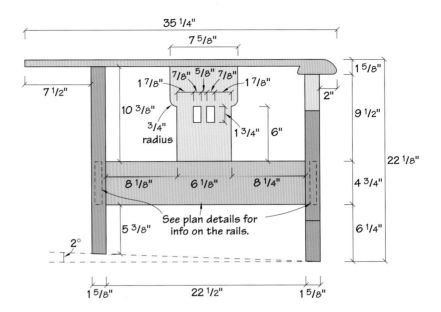

Profile

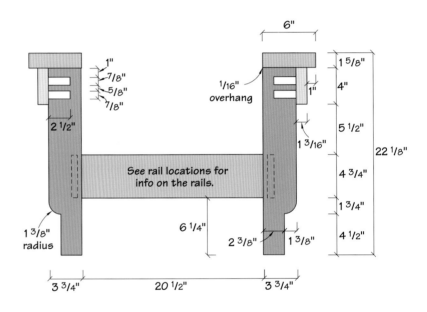

Elevation

Be sure to make a full-size mock-up of the legs and sides (top left) to determine the angle you need to cut on the bottom of the legs. When you determine that angle, use a grease pencil or felt-tip marker to paint the bottom of the legs. I cut the back and front legs simultaneously. Slowly inch your legs in after each cut until the color is all gone (bottom left).

To complete the legs, you need to cut the bottom of all four legs at a 2-degree angle so the chair sits flat on the floor. I recommend you make a full-size mock-up so you can get the angle exactly right. Cut the angle on a chop saw.

Assembly

Now you're almost ready to assemble the chair frame. You'll need to first miter the tenons slightly where they meet to fit in the mortises, using your table saw. Now finish sand everything. I went to 150-grit using my random orbit sander and hand sanded the whole piece with 180-grit. Yes, it makes a noticeable difference.

Now glue the front rail between the front legs and the back rail between the back legs. Clamp and allow your glue to dry. Use ¼" dowels to pin the tenons from the inside of the chair. This strengthens the weakest point of this chair. It's at this joint where the original

chair came loose.

Glue the side rails between the front and back legs and you can see your chair take shape.

Learn to Make Square Templates

Now you need to work on the arms. First glue the arm buildup pieces to the front of the arms. Then get ready to cut the mortises on the arms that will hold the tenons on the legs and side slats. A word of advice here: Mock up an arm out of scrap wood and practice on it first.

To make plywood templates for the mortises, you need to make a square hole in the middle of a piece of ply. The best way to do this is by making plunge cuts into your plywood on your table saw. Refer to the photo on page 25 to see how to do this.

Now cut your mortises. I used a template bit with cutters on the bottom and a guide bearing on top. If you don't have a bit with cutters on the bottom, you can still plunge with a straight bit. Just plunge slowly and wiggle the router a bit as you go. Cut the mortises in two passes.

After you're sure the arms fit on the legs, cut the curve on the front of the arm. Attach the full-size pattern to

your arm and cut the shape on a band saw. Clean up the cuts with a stationary belt sander. Now taper the arms with your band saw and clean up the cut with your jointer. Glue the arms and slats in place.

Now shape the back rod that adjusts the seat back angle. Bevel one edge of the rod on your jointer and cut notches on the ends so the rod fits between the arms. Attach the back to the seat frame with a piano hinge. Screw the cleats to the front and back of the frame in the locations shown in the diagram; slip the seat in place.

Finishing

This finish takes some effort, but it is well worth it. The first step is to dye the chair with an alcohol based aniline dye that's reddish. See the supplies list

for ordering information. Then apply one coat of boiled linseed oil to the chair. You can get this at any home-center store. Wipe off the excess and let it dry overnight. The linseed oil helps seal the wood before your final coloring step and helps bring out the ray flake.

Now wipe on a thin coat of Lilly's warm brown glaze. We live and die by this stuff when finishing Arts and Crafts furniture. We're not aware of a catalog that sells it, but you can visit Lilly's Web site (at the address in the supplies box) to find a paint store that carries this glaze. Wipe the glaze until you achieve an even tone. Allow it to dry overnight. Finally, apply three coats of a clear finish — whatever you're comfortable with.

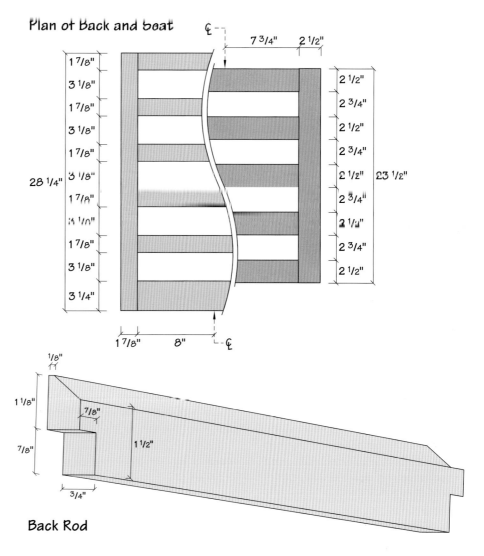

Plan of Back and Seat

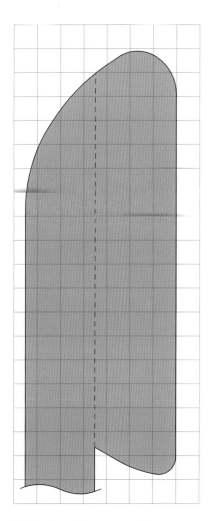

Full-size Diagram of Arm

Back Rod

This Arts and Crafts reproduction
will last a lifetime (or more).

Box Spindle Chair

GUSTAV STICKLEY IS KNOWN FOR QUALI-
TY ARTS AND CRAFTS DESIGNS, and this
Stickley-inspired box spindle chair is
no exception. The lack of through-
tenons in this design give the piece a
more contemporary appeal, while the
traditional quarter-sawn white oak (see
"What Is Quarter-sawing?" on page
123), pegged tenons and solid construction techniques make it true to
the original Arts and Crafts design.

The piece isn't very complicated,
but I won't tell you it can be built in a
weekend. There's a lot of repetitive
work in milling the many mortises and
tenons.

As mentioned, I used quarter-sawn
white oak for the chair, but I found it
difficult to purchase. Many local lum-
beryards don't get a lot of requests for
quarter-sawn white oak. They'll order
it, but you'll have to buy in quantity. If
you're looking for heavier stock (8/4,
10/4), you may find the search difficult
and the result pricey, but, as with the
mortises, the final result is worth the
extra effort.

Another option to purchasing 10/4
material is to use a process called
quadrilinear posts (a distinctive
Leopold Stickley construction technique) where four boards are mitered
and then glued around a center post.
This not only gives you the heavier
stock without the expense, but also displays the quarter-sawn faces with their
figured medullary rays on all four sides
of the legs.

Construction

Construction begins with preparing the
lumber according to the Schedule of
Materials. Take a few minutes to check
your table saw for square; this includes
blade setting, rip-fence-to-blade and
miter slots, and miter-gauge-to-blade.
Believe me, the last thing you want to
do is spend a lot of time cutting parts
and discover the whole thing's out of
square.

Once your material is milled, start
with the mortises in the legs. Each leg
will receive two ½"-wide by ⅞"-deep by
4"-long mortises for the stretchers between the inside faces of the legs.
These mortises start 10" up from the
bottom of each leg, so this is a good
time to determine the legs' orientation,
making sure the best quarter-sawn figure is seen. Clamp the legs together
with the bottoms flush, then mark the
mortise locations.

The rear legs will also receive two
½"-wide by ⅞"-deep by 1½"-long apron
mortises on the same faces as the
stretcher mortises. Start these mortises
¼" down from the top so the aprons will
be flush to the leg top. The front legs
receive only one apron mortise per leg,
located on the side facing the back legs.

I used a benchtop mortising machine
(Photo 1) to cut all the mortises on the
chairs, except for the through-mortises
in the arms. If you don't have a mortiser
and don't plan on getting one (this project is a great excuse to buy a new tool),
there are a number of other ways to

1 A benchtop mortiser makes the repetitive
work more manageable.

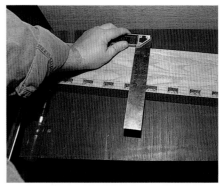

2 Time spent carefully laying out the mortise locations will pay big dividends during assembly.

produce the mortises. The traditional
method, for those of you who are
purists, is to mark and cut the mortises
by hand using a chisel. As it is, I don't
even have enough time to use the
power tools I have, so hand chopping 82
mortises wouldn't even be my second
choice. My preferred second method
would be to set up a jig for a plunge
router using a ½" bit. A couple of self-

centering router jigs are also available that are designed for making mortises, and as all of the mortises are in the centers of the pieces, this also would be a good alternative.

Once you've completed the leg mortises, move to the side stretchers and aprons and mark them for the 11 slats (Photo 2). Each slat will require a 1"-wide by ⅝"-deep mortise, so mark the mortise starting 1¼" in from each end (¾" allowance for the tenon), and at 1" intervals between. This will give you proper locations for the tenons and allow ¾" spacing between the slats.

Mark the back stretcher and apron similarly, but make the first mark 1¾" in from either end and then every inch.

Cutting the through-mortises in the arms will be among your final tasks, so you're through with mortises for now. The next step is to make all the tenons. Whichever piece you start with, the stretchers, aprons or slats, the process will be the same — three steps with dimension adjustments. Again, there's more than one way to make a tenon, but I used the basic table saw and a couple blocks of wood.

You'll get differing opinions as to which step of forming the tenon should be taken first. I prefer to form the cheeks first and define the shoulder last. This method prevents the saw-kerf from being visible on the shoulder — a big reason to do it this way! The other reason is to prevent a waste piece from being trapped by the blade and kicked back at you. In my preferred method, the waste on most of the pieces is all sawdust, so there's no concern about kickback.

I started with the slats and set my `rip fence for about ⅝" and the blade height for ⁷⁄₁₆". By running the slat through with one face against the fence, then turning it and running the opposite face against the fence, I was assured my tenon would be centered. Now the only trick left was to get a good fit in the mortise.

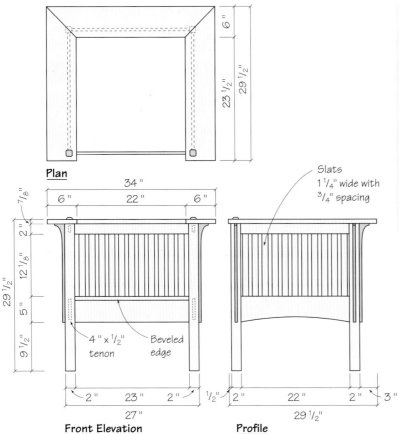

Plan

Front Elevation

Profile

Slats
1 1/4" wide with
3/4" spacing

4" x 1/2" tenon

Beveled edge

3 *A featherboard provides stability and safety while cutting the tenons.*

4 *A simple setup on the miter gauge makes cutting the tenons more consistent.*

5 *Use a stop block on the miter gauge to set the tenon shoulder depth.*

Once I was happy with the fit, I attached a featherboard to my saw. This kept my fingers away from the blade while making sure the slat didn't wobble during the cut, making the tenon too thin (Photo 3). Four passes on each slat, and I was headed to tenon heaven.

The next step is cutting the width of the tenons. I used the same rip fence setup method described above to determine the proper fit and center of the tenon, and then attached a board to my miter gauge to brace the slat against while making the cut. Photo 4 shows a second piece attached to the miter gauge to keep the slat tight against the rip fence. Note that the horizontal board attached to the miter gauge should be 1/16" to 1/8" away from the rip fence to avoid binding. With my miter gauge set up this way, it was fairly easy to run the four passes on each slat.

The last (and most important) cut for the tenons defines the shoulder. Again, you can use the rip fence and miter gauge for this step, or you can cut the shoulder depth using a stop block

clamped onto the miter gauge as shown in Photo 5. Make four passes on each piece, and then reset the blade depth and make the width passes.

Use these same steps to form the tenons on the stretchers and aprons. Pay attention to the last shoulder cut, as the waste piece can bind between the blade and the fence.

The through-tenons for the front legs are made last. Again, use the same three steps, with the final tenon size being 1½" × 1½" × 1". Remember, pay attention to the potential hazard of flying waste pieces.

Before you begin sanding, now is a good time to cut the profile on the corbels, or arm supports, and to cut the arch on the bottom of the side stretchers. Templates are provided for both on page 32. I used a band saw to make the cuts wide of the pencil lines, then sanded out much of the saw marks with a sanding drum chucked into my drill press. When you cut the corbels, you can interlock the pieces to waste as little wood as possible.

Working With An Upholsterer

If you're like most woodworkers, you use a needle only for splinter removal. So unless you're lucky enough to know a seamstress who can make the chair cushions, you'll need the services of an upholsterer.

I worked with Cincinnati upholsterer Jeff Rankin, involving him in the project from the beginning because I didn't want to overlook any details that were important to him. In a preliminary phone call I learned that a frame with webbing and a cushion 3" to 4" thick would establish my finished seat height. We

also determined the thickness of the back cushion, which is important in deciding the seat depth.

Fabric selection was the last question. Jeff suggested I'd save money by getting it myself. He simply advised me to buy 1½ yards of fabric, while he would supply the other materials.

Back at my shop, I completed the seat frame. Then I purchased the fabric and dropped it all off at Jeff's so we could review the job. I told him there was a ⅛" space allowance around the frame for fabric wrap-

ping; and we agreed that the cleats to support the frame wouldn't be installed until he completed his work.

You should know that if you're resourceful, you can do the upholstery work on the seat. The sewing for the back cushion is simpler than for most clothing. All the materials are readily available at fabric stores. If you hire the work done, as a benchmark, I paid $25 for the fabric and $75 for Jeff's time and materials.

—by Steve Shanesy

Photo A The seat cushion is shown upside down. Rubber webbing has been stapled in place on the frame. Strips of muslin have been glued to foam, which is cut 1" larger than the frame size.

Photo B The muslin has been pulled and stapled in place on the frame bottom. Begin pulling and fastening from the center of each side, then work toward the corners for consistency.

Photo C Right side up, the foam is formed by pulling and fastening muslin to give the cushion its final shape.

Photo E The back cushion is rectangular cut foam wrapped with fiberfill.

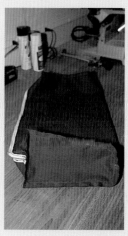

Photo F The zippered back fabric is sewn with separate end pieces to give it the proper angled shape of a bolster.

Photo D The upholstery fabric is stapled in place using the same method as the muslin. A layer of fiberfill is simply placed between the foam and fabric to give the cushion loft and smooth any irregularities. Fit the fabric in the corners neatly.

Do the final sanding for the curved edges with a random orbit sander. The most important consideration in forming the corbels is to make sure the top and glued edge form a square corner, and that a good jointer pass is left unsanded on the long edge.

Another detail prior to sanding is the 45-degree bevel on the top front edge of the front stretcher. Not only is this an attractive detail, but it also may keep your legs from going to sleep! I made the cut on the table saw, leaving

a ⅜" face on the top edge.

After you've sanded all the pieces, you're ready to assemble. Start with one set of side aprons and stretchers and 11 slats. Test the tenon fits for any problems, and use a chisel to adjust the fit if necessary. To assemble the side, I clamped the stretcher into my front bench vise and applied glue to all the mortises. Make sure you use enough glue, but remember that too much may keep the tenon from seating all the way in. My tenon fit was tight enough to re-

quire just a little persuasion with a dead-blow hammer, but if your tenons require more than a friendly tap, you risk bulging out the thin, ⅛" sides of the mortise.

After all the tenons are seated in the stretcher, remove the piece from the vise and place the apron in the same position. Start the first tenon into the mortise of the apron and tap it into place, then start the second, and so on, until all the tenons are started (Photo 6). Then either tap the tenons home, or

Enlarge 400% for full-size pattern.

Enlarge 200% for full-size pattern.

Important: By making these dimensions the same, the saw setup is the same for each dimension and therefore square! Always use these edges to fence.

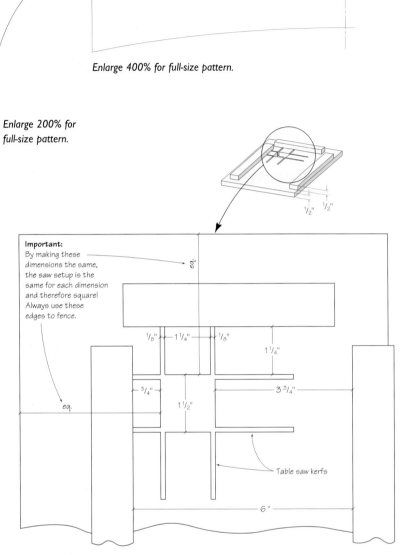

$^1/_8$" — 1$^1/_4$" — $^1/_8$"

1$^1/_4$"

$^3/_4$"

eq.

1$^1/_2$"

3$^3/_4$"

Table saw kerfs

6 "

Through-tenon Arm Jig (shown upside down)

Safety Tip

The center of a piece can be safely cut away (as with the arm jig) without cutting through the perimeter of the piece.

Mark the cutout location, then (with the blade stopped and lowered below table height) adjust the rip fence to place an edge of the cutout directly over the blade.

Turn the saw on and, while holding the piece down firmly (clear of the blade), slowly raise the blade up into the piece.

When the saw intersects the marked lines of the cutout, lower the blade (while still running) below table level; then turn the saw off. Repeat the steps to complete the cutout shape.

This tip is suggested for MDF or thin soft wood boards. Hard wood may cause dangerous kickbacks.

6 *The side assemblies should fit snugly, but if you force them, you'll split wood!*

7 *When attaching the legs to the side assembly, the best grain should face outward.*

8 *When drilling the peg holes, a piece of tape on the bit inexpensively controls depth.*

use a clamp to pull the assembly tight.

Next, dry fit the tenons of the assembled side into the mortises on the front and back legs. When the fit is good, apply glue to the mortises, assemble and clamp (Photo 7).

While the sides dry, drill the legs for pinning the tenons, then insert the pegs. I marked my $^1/_8$" drill bit with tape to keep the depth at 1$^1/_2$" and drilled two holes at each stretcher tenon and one hole at the apron tenon. The holes are drilled $^3/_8$" in from the edge and at the center of the apron tenon and 1" in

9 *Keep the saw blade parallel to the leg surface while cutting the peg flush.*

10 *Clamp diagonally across the chair frame, to adjust square to perfect.*

11 *Gluing on the corbels is fairly simple, but watch for glue squeeze-out.*

12 *A flush-cutting knife makes clean work of the through-mortise in the arm.*

13 *While gluing the arm assembly to the chair, you have another opportunity to check for squareness.*

from each stretcher tenon's width (Photo 8).

I cut my oak pegs to 2" lengths and then sanded a champfer on one end to allow it to slip into the hole easily. After putting a small amount of glue into the peg hole, I tapped the peg home, making sure the peg's end grain ran opposite the grain of the leg. Though this doesn't make the pegged joint any stronger, the greater contrast is attractive because it calls attention to the expressed joinery detail. The ½" of peg protruding from the hole is then trimmed flush to the leg (Photo 9) and sanded.

After the sides are dry, use the same procedure to assemble the rear slat assembly. Then glue it and the front stretcher between the sides and clamp (Photo 10). You should also check for square at this time, using a clamp to adjust.

The next step is to simply glue the corbels in place. The important factor is to center the corbel on the leg and keep the top flush with the leg top on the back leg and the tenon shoulder on the front leg (Photo 11).

Next, cut the chair arms and back cap to length, using a 45-degree miter joint for the back corners. The miter will be glued together using biscuits to align and strengthen the joint, but first cut the through-mortise for the front leg tenons.

First, make the router template shown in the plans. Use a table saw to make the cuts, and simply tack some ¾" × ¾" strips to the underside as indexing guides. These guides provide correct arm placement, while allowing you to

use only one clamp to hold the template in place during routing. (See the Safety Tip.)

I used a top-mounted bearing flush cutter in my router (Photo 12) so the size of the template opening is the same as the mortise. Once the template was complete, I fit it over one of the arms and marked the location of the mortise. Then I used a 1⅛" boring bit chucked into the drill press to clear away most of the waste from the hole before routing.

Unless you want to make two templates, you'll have to work from the underside of one of the arms, so pay attention to which side displays the best figure.

After clamping the template back on the arm, I then used the router to mill the rest of the mortise. I used a backing board to keep from cutting into the workbench top. The last step is to square out the mortises' corners using a chisel. Be careful with this — the top surface should mate exactly with the tenon.

Before gluing the mitered arms and back piece, I gently tapped the arms

into place over the tenons and marked the height of the arm on the tenon with a pencil. Next, I carefully removed the arms, and used a biscuit joiner and glue to fasten the mitered pieces together.

While these dried, I marked a ⅜" line around the top of the tenon, then used a random orbit sander to form a chamfer around the top of the tenon. This gives the chair an elegant finishing touch.

Once the arm assembly dries, apply glue to the entire top edge of the chair aprons and corbels and place the arms over the tenons. Before clamping, check the chair again for squareness; clamp the arms to the chair while adjusting for any unevenness (Photo 13).

The last two steps are to finish the piece and make the seat and back cushions (see "Working with an Upholsterer").

After that, the chair is ready to put to important work. Ease down, wiggle into a comfortable position ... read *Popular Woodworking* and plan your next project.

Just the right size for a lamp and a magazine,
this side table completes any seating area.

Spindle Side Table

THE MATCHING SIDE TABLE (OR TABORET) SHOWN IN THE PHOTO is an easy addition to the box spindle chair. The cutting sizes shown in the Schedule of Materials will allow you to assemble the table using mortise-and-tenon joints as found in the chair.

Begin by cutting the mortises in the legs using the steps described for the chair and the diagrams at right to locate the mortises. Once you've mortised the legs, mortise the stretchers and aprons to accept the five slats per side. The slats use the same ¾" spacing in between, but determine the location of the mortises from the center of the side rather than the edge.

Next cut the ½"-thick by 2½"-wide by ¾" long tenons on the ends of the stretchers and the ½"-thick by 1"-wide by ¼"-long tenons on the aprons. The final tenons are the ½"-thick by 1"-wide by ½"-long tenons on either end of the slats.

The arch on the underside of the stetcher is illustrated here. To assemble, place the slats into the apron and stretcher to form the slat assembly, then glue and clamp the assembly between two legs.

Once both side assemblies have dried, glue the two shorter aprons and the shelf between the two sides to form the table base. I added end caps to the shelf to give it a more massive appearance without increasing the material's thickness. You can use biscuits to attach the caps prior to assembly. Simply glue the shelf, or use a biscuit joiner to help alignment. The shelf sits between the legs and is set ¼" below the stretchers' top edge.

Fasten the top using cleats or other methods, but do not glue it to the base, as the top will expand and shrink with changes in humidity.

Schedule of Materials: Spindle Side Table

No.	Item	Dimensions T W L
4	Legs	1½" x 1½" x 26¼"
1	Top	¾" x 16" x 24 "
2	Stretchers	¾" x 3" x 18½"
2	Aprons	¾" x 1½" x 18"
2	Aprons	¾" x 1½" x 12"
10	Slats	⅝" x 1¼" x 8¾"
1	Shelf	⅝" x 11¾" x 15¾"
2	Shelf caps	⅝" x 1¼" x 11¾"

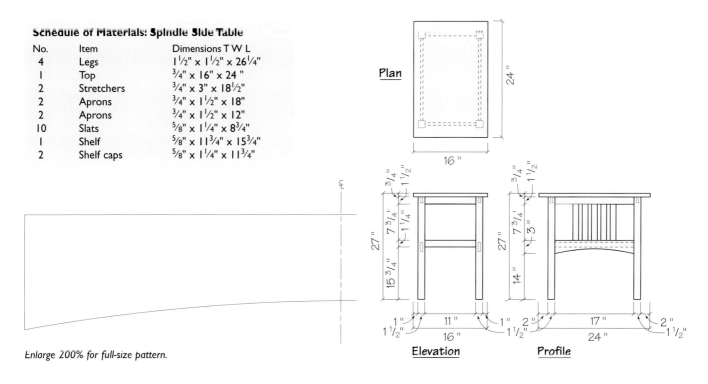

Enlarge 200% for full-size pattern.

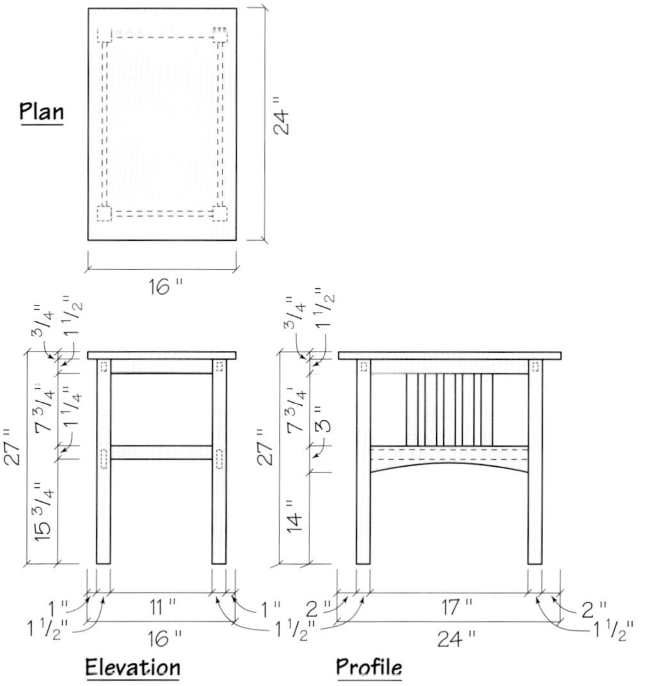

Comfort and unique style combine to make this rocker both a physical and a visual treat.

Inlaid Limbert Rocker

WHEN I WAS DECIDING WHICH ARTS AND CRAFTS ROCKER TO BUILD, I knew I wanted something a little lighter in looks than most recognized Arts and Crafts pieces. Many of the chairs in the Arts and Crafts style can look a little chunky and heavy for my taste. This chair caught my eye because it was lighter in design, but large enough to hold a big person comfortably and offer room for a little person to sit on your lap at story time. In addition, the inlays on the legs and curved arms, rockers and back rails are a good, but not overly difficult, building challenge. The original rocker was produced by the Limbert Furniture Company of Grand Rapids, Michigan, around 1910. Charles Limbert was a contemporary of Gustav Stickley, but much of his work added a slightly stylized appearance — he added cutouts, sweeps and inlays to separate his work from the more austere Arts and Crafts designs.

Design and Layout
All I had to reproduce the rocker was a black-and-white photograph from an auction catalog, so I ended up using a scale ruler to determine the dimensions. I took those dimensions and drew a full-scale side elevation and a top plan drawing of the chair. I've created drawings like this for over 20 years for every detailed piece of furniture that I have made. The drawings help answer questions about construction and what joints to use, and allow me to actually

build the piece in my head as I draw it. The drawing process also allows me to make mistakes that a simple eraser can correct! During building, I constantly refer to the construction drawings so I can keep the project clear in my head. I suggest you take the information from the Schedule of Materials and the diagrams and make your own full-size elevation and plan-view drawings.

Building the Legs
My first construction decision was to choose quarter-sawn white oak as my material. This is true to the original piece, but cherry would also fit into this style. Start your cutting with the legs. The front legs are square and easy to cut out. Remember to orient your wood with the most attractive face forward. The back legs require a routing template. Start by using the band saw to rough-cut a blank for each back leg. Next, lay out a ⅛"-thick template for the back leg shape using the dimensions given in the scaled diagrams. At tach the template to the leg blank with flathead screws on the *inside* of each leg at the areas where the mortises will be cut at the bottom. Also put screws where the two back rails will be attached at the top of the leg. Those screw holes will be covered by the back rails when the chair is assembled. Use a router with a flush-cutting routing bit to shape each leg. Be sure to make one right and one left leg.

Routed Inlays

Lay out the location for the inlays on the front faces of each leg. Start the inlay work by routing the long, straight channels first (Photo 1). Rout the channel ⅛" deep using a ¼"-wide straight bit in a plunge router. I used an edge guide set to center the channel from either side of the leg. Next, cut the inlay material (in my case, some scrap moradillo I had lying around, but walnut would work well, also), ¼" thick. I cut the inlay width a bit on the snug side and final-fit it with my hand plane.

To glue the inlay in place, put glue into the groove, insert the inlay, and then use a caul and clamps to *press* (not hammer) the inlay into place. Set these pieces aside to dry for several hours or overnight. By doing this, all the moisture will be gone from the glue and the wood will be back to its normal moisture content. Then level the inlay flush to the leg with a plane. I used a mortising machine to create the square holes at the ends of inlays, but a router and a template will work just as well (Photo 2). You'll need to square the corners with a chisel if you use a router.

Laminated Bending

Now comes the fun part! Bending. All the radii are the same, so you have to make only one bending jig. (Medium-density fiberboard (MDF) makes a stable and affordable bending jig.) The longest bent pieces are the rockers, so cut the six ¾"-thick jig pieces about 42" long and 8" deep. Next, use a set of trammel points to strike the radius (shown on the diagram) on one of the MDF blanks. Rough-cut to the outside of the line and then sand to the line. Then use a flush-trim router bit and this first jig plate to create the radius on the other five plates.

Lamination bending is just that — thin strips of wood bent over a form and glued together to form a bent piece of wood. This is a good way to bend wood because it remains stable, the grain patterns of the original face can be kept when bent, and the final lamination is strong.

Start the lamination process by cut-

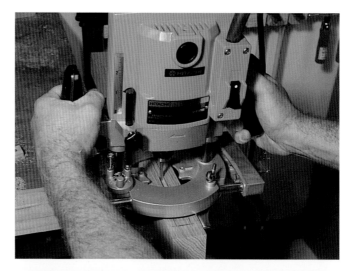

1 Use a router with an edge guide to rout the ¼"-wide channel for the inlay.

2 The square ends of the inlays can be done with a mortiser as shown here, or you can use a router with a template and use a chisel to square out the corners.

3 When doing lamination bending, you will have lots of glue squeeze-out. This tells you that all surfaces will be bonded well after the glue dries. Note the jig segments. These can be removed as needed for narrower pieces.

ting blanks for the rockers, arms and back rails ¼" wider than the finished dimensions in the Schedule of Materials. Resaw the blanks into strips a little thicker than ⅛". Keep the pieces in order as they come off the band saw. I used the old woodworker's "triangle" drawn on the edges of the blanks to keep the strips in order. (By marking a triangle across pieces that will be glued back together, you get an obvious "up" and "down" for the piece, as well as defining the order of the pieces.) Thickness sand these pieces to ⅛". You could also use a thickness planer, taking light passes.

How to Glue Up

At glue-up time, have your clamps ready to go! Be sure to wax or seal all the surfaces on the jig that will come into contact with glue, so the dried glue can be easily removed. Lay out the strips in order and apply yellow wood glue to each strip. I use a brush, and cover every square inch of the wood face with glue. (I thin the glue with a little water to make it easier to spread with a brush. Thinning doesn't affect the holding power of the glue.)

Move quickly and put the strips together. Then place the whole assembly on the form with a ¼"- to ⅜"-thick piece of plywood to serve as a caul to even out the clamping pressure. Put your first clamp in the middle of the jig, then work your way out from the middle, applying clamps as needed (Photo 3). You will have glue run-out everywhere. That's a good sign that all surfaces are bonding! (See Photo 3.) Leave the clamps on for at least two hours.

Gluing the Back Rails

Since the back rails are 3½" wide, I used only five plates for the bending jig. (It makes it easier to put the clamps on both sides of the jig to get an even clamping pressure.) You'll need seven ⅛"-thick strips for each of the rails. Apply glue and put the rail assembly on the jig in the center. Again, put the first clamp in the center of the assembly and work your way out to either end. When the rail blanks are dry, scrape the glue off of one edge and use a jointer to flat-

4 The arms are half curved and half straight. Clamp the straight part first and then clamp the curved part using the end of the jig.

ten and square that edge. Then cut the blanks to 3½" wide using the table saw. Set these aside for now.

Gluing and Cutting the Rockers

The rockers are 2¼" wide, so I left four plates in the jig. I used 10 strips for each rocker. Glue up as before, starting from the center when clamping. When the glue is dry, square and cut the rockers to width. Lay the rockers on the full-size drawings and mark the angles on each end. Cut these angles on the table saw using a miter gauge with a 40° wooden fence attached. Hold the rocker on its side, tightly against the fence with the curve arching away from your body. Adjust the miter-gauge angle until it matches the angle you want to cut on the end of the rocker. Do this for both ends of the rockers, then set them aside for now.

Gluing the Arms

Each arm requires seven ⅛" by 4½"-wide strips, so I used all six of the bending jigs. The arms have a radius only on the back half of the arms, so I used 13" at one end of the radius jig. Half of the arm was on the jig, and half was sandwiched between two straight boards used as cauls. I found it helpful to glue up the straight part first and then quickly move this all to the end of the jig (Photo 4). You might need an assistant to help hold all of this together.

When the arms are dry, scrape the

glue off of one edge, joint that edge, then cut the blanks to 4¼" wide on the table saw.

Seat Rails and Back Slats

The rails and slats are straight-ahead solid wood pieces. Size them as given in the Schedule of Materials. While you're cutting square wood, also machine and cut the seat slats and cleats. The curves on the bottom of the seat rails will be cut after the tenons are cut on the rails.

Mortises and Tenons

As with most solid chairs, the secret to longevity is in the joinery. One of the best possible chair joints is a mortise and tenon. Using the diagrams, lay out the ½" × 5" × ¹⁵⁄₁₆" mortises for the seat rails on the front and back legs. I used a benchtop mortising machine to drill my mortises, but a drill press or router will work in a pinch.

Next cut ½" × 5" × ⅞" tenons on both ends of the seat rails. I used my table saw and miter gauge to do this step, first defining the shoulder at ⅞" using the rip fence as a stop. My first pass was on the 6" faces, with the blade height set for ³⁄₁₆". I then reset the height to ½" and ran the ⅞"-wide faces. With the shoulders defined, I reset the rip fence for ¹¹⁄₁₆" and ran the rails upright, with the 5" face against the fence. Check the tenon fit, then use your miter gauge again to cut the tenons to 5" wide. Where the tenons meet at the corner of the leg mortises, you need to cut a 45-degree bevel on the ends of the tenons.

The back rails are held in place with a manufactured mortise-and-tenon joint — better known as a dowel. To determine the length of the back rails between the legs, I measured the distance from cheek to cheek on the back seat rail. To cut the back rails to length, I first found the center of the rail blanks. Using the measurement I got from the back seat rail, I worked from the center mark on the back rail and marked the length to cut the rail.

To cut the curved rails so they would fit well against the back legs, I laid the rail (convex side down) against the miter-gauge fence. I then put a spacer under the rail (between the blade and the center point of the rail), to support the rail as I made the cut. This cut is safe as long as you adequately support the rail during the cut. Expect a little tear-out on the underside of the cut, so take your cut slowly. Turn the rail and cut the other end the same way. Cut the other rail to match the first.

With the back rails cut to length, it's time to lay out the mortises for the slats on the upper and lower back rails. Start by spacing the slats equally along the rail. The mortises will be cut straight and the rail is obviously curved, so using a fence as a guide won't work. Draw ¼" × 3¼" mortises centered on the rail.

To cut the ⅜"-deep mortises in the back rails, I again used the mortising machine, but without a fence. I cut the mortises freehand by using the straight lines as a guide. The mortise needs to be tight, not pretty, because the shoulder of the slat tenon will hide the mortise. With a little patience, this process worked well. A drill press would also work for this operation.

Using the same dimensions as the back-rail mortise, cut the mortises in the two seat side-rails for the side slats.

Cut the tenons on all the back slats and just the bottom tenons on the side slats. The tenons on the tops of the side slats will be cut later.

5 *Use a pattern to trace the layout of the arm. The tenon and wraparound can be made by using the band saw to cut away most of the waste. Use a chisel and file to make the final shape. Check the fit to the back leg as you progress.*

6 *A router with a guide bushing and a template works very well for making the through-mortise on the arm. Use a file to square out the corners.*

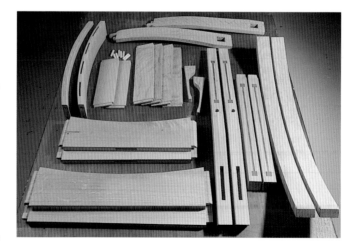

7 *These are the parts ready to be sanded.*

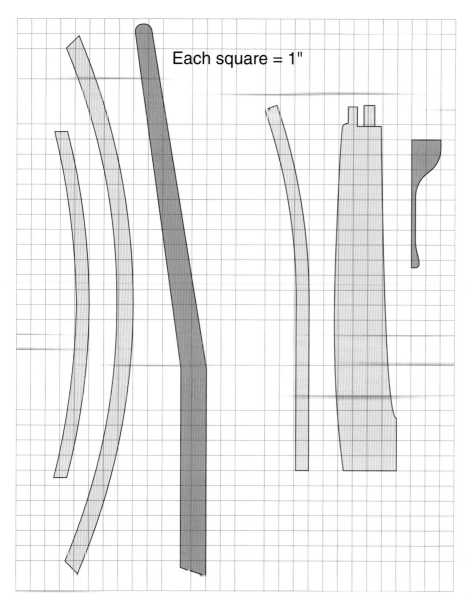

Each square = 1"

Dry Fitting the Chair

This is a good point to dry fit the chair and get a look at how it is all going to go together. It's also a good chance to think through the order of assembly. The two front legs and front seat rail form a sub-assembly. The two back legs, the back seat rail, the two back rails and the four slats form another subassembly. These two subassemblies are joined to one another with the two side seat rails.

While the chair is clamped together dry, put the back-rail/back-slat assembly in place between the back legs and clamp it with enough pressure to hold it in place. Adjust the fit of the back slat section to its finished position, and mark the top and bottom back rail locations on the back legs. This will give you your dowelling locations.

Dowelling the Back Rails

Using the marks made on the back legs, mark the two back rails for two ⅜" dowels in each end. It's easy to drill the dowel locations in the rails freehand (rather than making a jig) to keep them perpendicular to the end faces of the rails. Reassemble the back-rail/back-slat assembly and use dowel centers to locate the dowel locations in the back legs. Use a drill press to drill the holes in the back legs, then put it all back together again to check the fit.

Fitting the Arms

I used the photo in the auction catalog to determine how the arms would fit into the front and back legs. Refer to the scaled diagram of the rear part of the arm and make a full-size paper or cardboard template. Square over the front of the arms on the table saw, then lay the template square to the front of each arm. Trace the pattern onto the blanks, remembering to make right and left arms.

Cut out the arms on the band saw, leaving the pencil marks, then sand to the pencil marks. Don't cut the tenon and "wraparound" on the back of the arm yet. Instead, just leave the arm about ½" long. By holding the arm blank alongside the front leg and the side of

Schedule of Materials: Inlaid Limbert Rocker

No.	Lett.	Item	Dimensions T W L	Species
2	A	Front legs	1¾" x 1¾" x 22¼"	QSWO
2	B	Back legs	1¾" x 5" x 36⅝"	QSWO
2	C	Rockers	1¼" x 2¼" x 35¾"	QSWO
2	D	Seat rails f&b	⅞" x 6" x 24¾"	QSWO
2	E	Seat rails side	⅞" x 6" x 20¾"	QSWO
2	F	Back rails	⅞" x 3½" x 23"	QSWO
2	G	Corbels	⅞" x 2" x 8½"	QSWO
2	H	Seat cleats	⅞" x ⅞" x 23"	Maple
2	I	Seat cleats	⅞" x ⅞" x 18¹⁄₁₆"	Maple
5	J	Seat slats	⅞" x 3½" x 19⅞"	Maple
2	K	Arms	⅞" x 4⅜" x 24⅛"	QSWO
4	L	Back slats	⅜" x 3½" x 16"	QSWO
2	M	Side slats	⅜" x 3½" x 12⁵⁄₁₆"	QSWO

QSWO = quarter-sawn white oak

the dry-assembled chair, I was able to mark the arms to length and where they would join the back legs, and trace the angle of the arm onto the legs.

With the arm location and angle marked, drill a ¾" hole in each back leg, matching the angle of the arm. Next, cut the arms to length, notching for the dowel and wraparound. Use the band saw and some handwork to shape the wraparound and round tenon on the ends of the arms to fit the ¾" hole in the legs (Photo 5).

With the chair still dry fit, put the arms in place allowing the shoulder of the round-tenon joint to flush to the back leg of the chair. Then measure the distance from the back leg to the top of the front leg and transfer this measurement to each arm. Use this location to mark where the through-mortise is to be cut for the front leg's through-tenon.

Use a router, template guide and a simple plywood template (Photo 6) to cut the through-mortise, squaring the corners with a file and chisel afterward. To mark the top of the front leg, use the through-mortise, and set your table saw to cut the tenon 1" long on the leg. About ⅛" of the leg tenon should show on the top of the arm. Cut the peak on the front leg with the blade on the table saw set at 7 degrees.

With the chair again dry-assembled, fit the arms to the front and back legs. Then mark the underside of the arms for the slat mortises. Cut this ¼" × 3" × ½"-deep mortise freehand as described earlier with the back slats. Then scribe the curve of the underside of the arm to the top edge of the side slat (leave ½" for the tenon) and cut the curve on the band saw. Next, cut the tenon on the table saw to match the curve of the end. Cut out the corbels on the band saw using the template in the diagrams. Then do one more dry-fit to final check all the parts, and you're ready to start sanding.

Sanding and Finishing

Sand all parts to 150-grit with a random orbit sander. If you've ever tried to apply stain or finish to a piece of furni-

8 A ¾" dowel with slots and wedges will hold the rockers in place for many years to come.

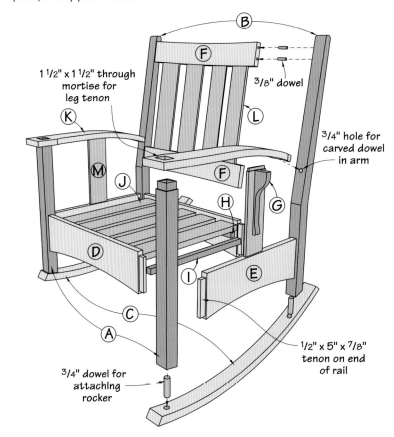

1½" x 1½" through mortise for leg tenon

3/8" dowel

3/4" hole for carved dowel in arm

1/2" x 5" x 7/8" tenon on end of rail

3/4" dowel for attaching rocker

ture with lots of angles and joints, you know runs and blotches are a concern. I chose to finish all of the pieces prior to assembly, taping off all the glue joint areas. I first applied a gel stain with a predominantly red tint, wiping the stain to an even color. I then applied a medium brown glaze, wiping it to an even

color I liked. I let this all dry for four hours, then sprayed on three coats of pre-catylized lacquer, sanding between coats with 320-grit sandpaper.

After allowing the finish to cure overnight, I assembled the chair. To secure the rockers, I used a 2½" × ¾" dowel slotted on both ends at right angles to each other to accept wedges. The first wedge is put into a slot and cut so ⅛" is left sticking out. When the dowel is driven into the hole with the slot and wedge going into the hole first the wedge will be forced into the slot and will spread the dowel inside the hole in the leg, locking it into place. Another wedge is put into the other slot and driven home to hold the rocker in place (Photo 7).

For additional holding power where the arms join the back legs, I drilled a pilot hole into the back of the leg and put a screw into the tenon on the arm. I plugged the hole with the same wood used for the inlaid parts of the chair (Photo 8).

Seat and Back Cushions

The seat is a 6"-thick, firm, foam pad with a sewn upholstery cover. The back pad measures about 2" thick, is filled with a batting material and hangs over the back rail of the chair on straps which button to the back of the cushion.

Once you finish this great project, you'll have a beautiful Arts and Crafts piece, as well as a nice place to sit and just "rock-on."

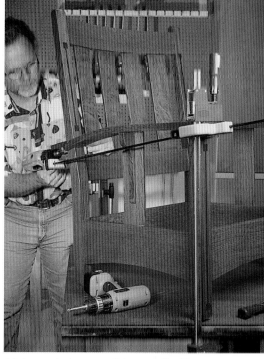

9 *A screw in the tenon of the arm will add extra strength to the back of the chair. The hole can be plugged with the same wood used in the inlays.*

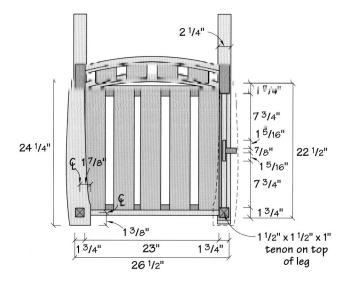

Elevation

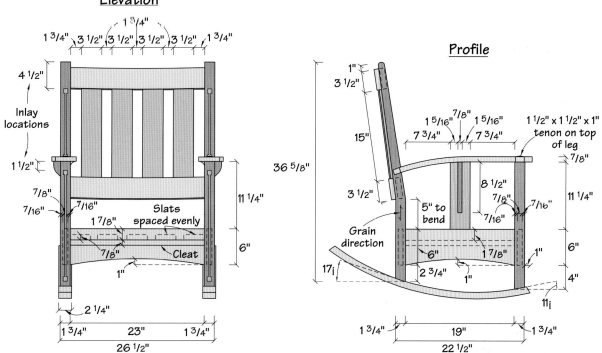

Profile

Benefiting from a heavy dose of Asian influence, this entry bench from the Blacker House shows the movement at its most graceful.

Greene & Greene Entry Bench

THIS WILL UPSET SOME OF THE PURISTS OUT THERE, but I think that some of the best designs in the Arts and Crafts style come from the fringes of the movement. Instead of Gustav Stickley's massive and square forms, I prefer Art Nouveau–influenced furniture from Scotsman Charles Rennie Mackintosh. And instead of the squarish Lifetime Furniture, I've always liked the Asian influence in the furniture and architecture of Charles and Henry Greene.

This bench from the Brothers Greene was designed and built in 1907 for the Robert R. Blacker house in Pasadena, California. The story behind this house is a sad one. As the furniture

designed for the house went out of style, most of it was sold at a yard sale in 1947. Then, in 1985, the house was purchased and within three days was stripped of most of its lighting fixtures, stained glass windows and door transoms. These were sold piecemeal to collectors all over the world, quickly recouping the $1 million price of the house. Though new owners have taken possession of the house and a strong effort is being made to reclaim the original pieces, many can be seen only in photos or as reproductions.

This bench is as faithful to the original as I could manage, including the reedlike design of the back slats that lends a lightness not often seen in the Arts and Crafts style. The construction is a blend of modern and traditional. And while the original was made of teak, I chose cherry.

The Case of the Chair
Because this project is a mix of case construction and chair building, you'll use techniques from both disciplines.

Who Were the Greenes?
Charles Sumner Greene (1868–1957) and Henry Mather Greene (1870–1954) designed some of the most sought-after houses and custom furniture in the Pasadena, California, area. The brothers were born in the Midwest, and studied woodworking, metalworking and toolmaking at Washington University in St. Louis. After studying architecture at the Massachusetts Institute of Technology and a short stint as apprentices to other architects, Charles and Henry moved to Pasadena and set up their own architectural firm. On their trip west, the two stopped at the Columbian Exposition in Chicago and saw Japanese architecture for the first time, which greatly influenced both brothers.

Unlike many of their Arts and Crafts contemporaries, the Greene brothers designed furniture and interiors using teak and mahogany instead of quarter-sawn white oak. Their work also has a decidedly Japanese flavor not found in the works of Gustav Stickley and the Roycrofters.

The Greene brothers' most famous design is the Gamble House in Pasadena. Commissioned in 1908 by David Berry Gamble (of Procter & Gamble fame), the house was once in danger of being sold to a family that planned to paint the stunning mahogany and teak interiors white. The house is now operated as a museum.

45

The templates for the slats are provided on the scaled-down grids. After enlarging them, lay out the templates on your wood, cut the tenons on the end of the board and band saw the slats to shape.

While the slats can be sanded smooth, I find that a spokeshave helps remove irregularities left by the band saw. It also gives the piece a hand-worked appearance.

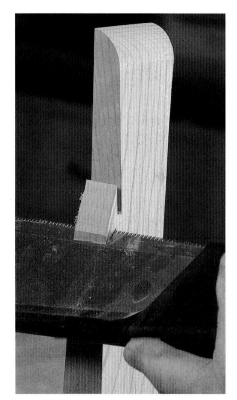

Notching the back leg to fit the back rail is a little tricky, so take the time to do it right. This joint is one of the most noticed features of the piece.

The most difficult step is getting the joint between the back legs and top rail right. It's a specialized coped miter that requires patience.

Begin construction by cutting the parts according to the Schedule of Materials. The front legs can be cut from 8/4 material, while the back legs are cut from a laminated blank glued up using scarf joints. I used three pieces of 8/4 cherry for each back leg, with the back section cut from the longest piece to avoid showing a visible seam. Start shaping the legs by cutting the profile first. Cut the top radius on the back leg after the back is assembled. Next, cut the outside radius of each back leg on the elevation face. Before cutting the curve on the inside edge, lay out and cut the coped miter for the top rail according to the diagram. The straight inside edge gives a better reference for laying out the coped miter. Then rout a ¼" radius on the visible corners of all the legs. Now cut out the arms on the band saw.

To form the storage area, the box ends need a 6-degree bevel on the front and back edges, and a ¼" × ¼" groove for the bottom that's cut ½" up from the lower inside edge. The same groove is necessary on the front and back box pieces. After making these cuts, mark and cut biscuit slots to attach the front and back legs to the box ends. Make the slots to hold the end panels recessed ½" in from the outside of each leg.

The next step is to cut a ¼" × ¾" tenon on the top end of the boards from which the slats will be cut. On the bottom end of the boards, cut a 7-degree bevel to allow the slats to lean to the back, so the long part of the bevel should face forward. Next, cut out the slat shapes on a band saw and use a scroll saw for the centers of the two spade-shaped slats. Then clean up the rough edges with a spokeshave.

Making Ends Meet

You're now ready to dry assemble the bench frame. Use biscuits again to at-

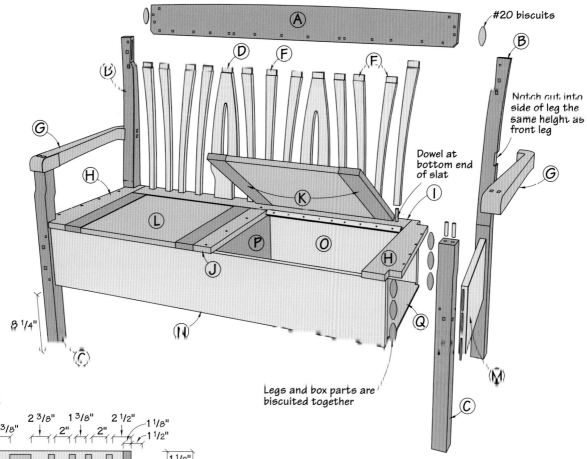

#20 biscuits

Notch cut into side of leg the same height as front leg

Dowel at bottom end of slat

Legs and box parts are biscuited together

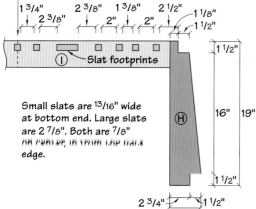

8 1/4"

Slat footprints

1 3/4"   2 3/8"   1 3/8"   2 1/2"
   2 3/8"   2"   2"   1 1/8"
                                1 1/2"

1 1/2"

16"   19"

1 1/2"

2 3/4"   1 1/2"
   4 1/4"

Small slats are 13/16" wide at bottom end. Large slats are 2 7/8". Both are 7/8" at point of trim the back edge.

Plan of seat frame end "H" and slat layout on seat frame back "I"

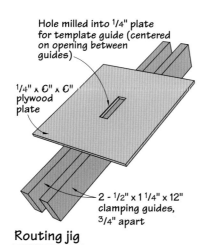

Hole milled into 1/4" plate for template guide (centered on opening between guides)

1/4" x 6" x 6" plywood plate

2 - 1/2" x 1 1/4" x 12" clamping guides, 3/4" apart

Routing jig

Schedule of Materials: Greene & Greene Entry Bench

No.	Ltr.	Item	Dimensions T W L	Material
1	A	Top rail	3/4" x 4 5/8" x 45 1/2"	Cherry
2	B	Back legs *	2 3/4" x 4 3/8" x 40"	Cherry
2	C	Front legs	1 3/4" x 2 1/8" x 23 3/4"	Cherry
2	D	Large slats	5/8" x 4 1/4" x 18 1/4"	Cherry
10	E	Small slats	5/8" x 2 1/4" x 18 1/4"	Cherry
1	F	Center slat	5/8" x 1 1/2" x 18 1/4"	Cherry
2	G	Arms	1 3/4" x 2" x 20 1/8"	Cherry
2	H	Seat frame ends	3/4" x 4 1/4" x 19"	Cherry
1	I	Seat frame back *	3/4" x 3 1/2" x 41 3/8"	Cherry
1	J	Seat frame center	3/4" x 2 1/2" x 15 1/2"	Cherry
4	K	Bread board ends †	3/4" x 2 1/2" x 15 1/2"	Cherry
2	L	Lids †	11/16" x 15 1/2" x 14 7/16"	Cherry
2	M	Box ends	3/4" x 8" x 16 3/16"	Cherry
1	N	Box front	3/4" x 8" x 46 7/8"	Cherry
1	O	Box back	3/4" x 8" x 43 5/8"	Cherry
1	P	Divider	3/4" x 7 1/4" x 17"	Cherry
1	Q	Bottom	1/4" x 17 1/2" x 48 1/2"	Plywood

* Rough length
† Requires fitting after assembly
5/16" x 5/16" x 30" and 7/16" x 7/16" x 20" of ebony plug material
1- Antique-brass continuous hinge 1 1/2" x 48" cut into 19" lengths

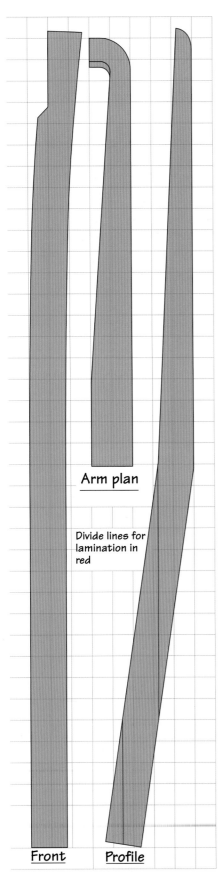

Arm plan

Divide lines for
lamination in
red

Front   Profile

Front/profile of back leg
and arm plan

Each square = 1"

tach the box front and box back between the legs. Make sure the angles are correct and the bottom fits. Then cut the top rail to length and clip the corners at a 45-degree angle to fit between the legs and biscuit it in place.

The next step is to notch the back legs for the arms. Use the front legs as a guide. The notch is ¼" deep by the size of the arm's end. Mark and drill for dowels to attach the arms to the top of the front leg. Also drill clearance holes in the back legs to screw the rear of the arm to the back leg from the inside of the leg. With the bench still dry assembled, go ahead and lay out and drill ⅜" dowel holes for the slats.

After resolving any fitting problems, cut a ¼" × ¾" groove into the center of the bottom edge on the top rail. This will hold the slats' tenons. Then actually glue the bench together. Start by nailing the divider in place between the box front and back, holding the top edges flush. Then put glue on the biscuits and

fit the legs onto the box parts, fitting the slats and top rail in place at the same time. There are a lot of pieces to align, but the glue will allow you about five minutes to check the slats before it starts to set.

The next step is to assemble and attach the seat frame. Biscuit the back and center pieces together, and then nail the frame in place to the assembled box. After everything is dry, cut the radius on the top rail and leg ends. Rout a ¼" radius on all the edges of the top rail and smooth it out.

Breadboards and Lift Lids

The last step in assembling the bench is to make the lift lids with breadboard ends. These provide a seat and lid for the storage area below. Begin by gluing up two panels for the lids. Breadboards have been around for hundreds of years as a means of stabilizing a panel as it goes through seasonal humidity changes. Breadboards can be made in

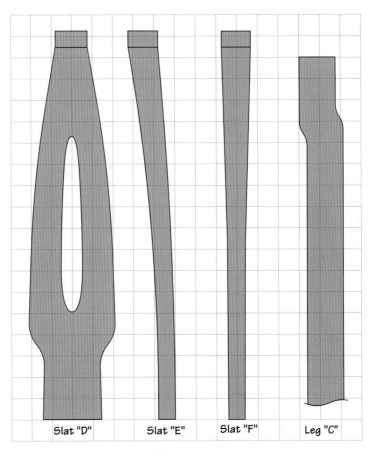

Slat "D"   Slat "E"   Slat "F"   Leg "C"

Back slats and leg profile

Each square = 1"

I made a simple mortising jig to help with the breadboards. Once the three-piece jig is done, a plunge router makes simple work of the mortises.

With the mortises cut in the breadboard ends, cut an elongated clearance hole at the bottom of the mortise. Then screw the breadboards in place and cap them with the rectangular plugs as shown.

many ways that involve complicated joinery, I chose a method that is simple and gives an authentic look. Rout three mortises in each breadboard 1"-deep by 1⅛"-long. Use a chisel to square out the mortises. The breadboard ends are a little long, so cut them to length after attaching them to the panel with no. 10×3" pan head screws. When you're happy with the fit of the breadboards, tap fitted plugs in place with glue. Trim and sand the plugs flush. Attach the lids to the bench with continuous hinges.

Planting the Plugs

The finishing accent for this piece, and one that is a trademark of the Greene & Greene style, is to add ebony plugs to many of the bench joints. See the box on the right for a handy way to do this. Adding color to this bench isn't terribly difficult, although it does take a little patience. First color the wood with Moser's Light Sheraton Mahogany dye, available from Woodworkers Supply (800) 645-9292, item #W13304, $11.90 for 4 ounces of powder. Allow it to dry. Apply one coat of clear finish. Then wipe on warm brown glaze (available at professional paint stores) and wipe the bench with your rag until most of the bench is colored evenly. Allow that to dry overnight. Then complete the process with two coats of a clear finish.

Square Plugs and Square Holes Made Simple

There doesn't seem to be any rhyme or reason to the plug locations used by Greene & Greene, except that the plugs were symmetrical. Used ostensibly to hide screws, nails and other fasteners, plugs should be at all of the major joint locations. There are two sizes of plugs, ⁵⁄₁₆" square and ⁷⁄₁₆" square. This is the fastest and easiest way to do this:

If there's a nail in the location of the plug, set it as deeply as you can.

Now drill a hole (either ⅜" or ¼" in diameter) that's about ⅜" deep.

Now square the hole. I bought inexpensive steel bar stock from my local home center (⁷⁄₁₆" square and ⁵⁄₁₆" square). Then I tapered one end on my grinder. Tap the bar stock into your round hole and it will become a square hole.

Put a small dot of glue in the hole and tap your ebony plug in place.

Use a piece of cardboard as a spacer between your work and a flush-cutting saw. Cut the plug and sand it slightly so there's still a raised bump.

Octagonal Taboret

IF YOU'VE NEVER SEEN ONE OF THESE LITTLE TABLES FOR SALE, you're in for a big shock. I first saw a taboret like this buried under a heap of junk in a small antique shop in Tallahassee, Florida, in 1990. It was about 20" high, signed by L. & J.G. Stickley and about $1,500 over my budget. And that Florida table wasn't an overpriced aberration. In 1996, tables like this were selling at auction in Chicago for between $800 and $1,500.

However, you can build one of these highly desirable tables in quarter-sawn white oak for about $75. Or you can buy ash, another wood commonly used for these tables, and spend about $40. We used quarter-sawn white oak because we thought the exceptional ray flake (technically called medullary rays) in the oak was worth the extra cost.

The design for this table is based on several originals. The splayed legs are inspired by a similar table built by the Charles P. Limbert Company. The graceful tapering of the legs can be found in pieces built by the Tobey Furniture Company. And the table's top, whether octagonal or round, can be found on pieces made by many manufacturers, including Gustav Stickley and Stickley Brothers.

We also decided to make the table a knockdown piece. Many pieces of Arts and Crafts furniture could be easily disassembled this way for delivery by train, which saved significantly on shipping costs. This table can be taken apart and mailed in a small box, which makes it a great gift because the whole thing can be assembled in about five minutes using only a screwdriver.

Prepare the Top

Begin by choosing the boards for the top and legs and cutting the material to rough size. We tried to pick boards that had the most dramatic ray flake and curl for the highly visible parts, but quartersawn oak can be tricky. What looks dramatic in the rough can look mundane after finishing.

The 20" top is made from two or three boards glued along their edges. It's a good idea to try several different arrangements of the top pieces before gluing to get the best grain pattern.

Once the glue is dry (a couple hours should be sufficient), cut the top to its desired shape. We used a circle-cutting jig with a band saw to cut the round top and trammel points to lay out the octagonal top (see "Lay Out an Octagon" for information on an easy method). Flatten the top with a cabinet scraper, if you have one, or a belt sander followed by a random orbit sander. To give the top a thinner look, cut a ⅛" chamfer on the top's edge using a router and a chamfer bit.

The Big Mortises

Cut the large ¾" × 3" mortises in the legs for the bottom stretchers by first chain-drilling a series of holes. The trick here is to drill the mortises at an 8-degree angle to match the angle of

Lay Out an Octagon

This method goes back to the time of Pythagoras and the ancient Greeks. All you need is a trammel, a straightedge and a surface to work on. First, cut the top square. Next, determine the center of the top by drawing intersecting lines with a straightedge, from opposite corners, across the top. Set your trammel points to make a mark as long as the distance from the center to an outside corner. Put the pin in one corner. Pivoting from the corner, draw a radius where it intersects with the square along the two adjacent sides. Repeat for all corners. Connect the marks.

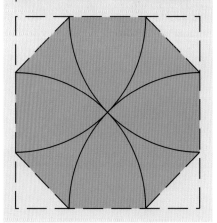

the legs that taper in toward the top. These mortises are centered on the leg, and the bottom edge is 5" up from the bottom of the leg.

Smaller Mortises

Cut the ¾" × 1¼" mortises for the top stretchers are cut in the legs in a similar fashion, ½" down from the top. However, for these cuts you'll need a fence fastened in the opposite direction as used on the large mortises to accommodate the vertical rather than horizontal mortises.

Clean Your Mortises

Because these mortises will be visible when the piece is finished, clean up the chain-drilled mortises. Use a 1" chisel to remove the waste on the long sides and a ½" chisel on the shorter sides. A mallet is handy for starting your cuts.

Bevel the Leg Ends

Because the legs cant slightly toward the top of the table, you need to bevel the top and bottom edges of each leg. This allows the leg bottom to sit flat on the floor and the tabletop to rest flat on the legs.

Taper the Legs

The graceful taper of the legs makes this hefty oak piece appear a little lighter. While you could use a tapering jig on your table saw, we decided to make the cuts on the band saw. After we cut the taper on both sides (cutting a little wide of the line), we ran the edges on a jointer to clean up the cuts.

Then, to give the legs even less heft, we routed a ⅛" chamfer on the long front edges of all four legs. This chamfer is quite common on many Arts and Crafts–style pieces.

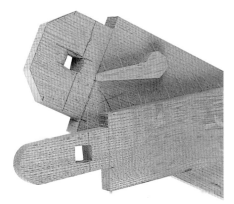

Make these mortises with a ½" bit in your drill press. Then square the corners with a chisel. The wedges are made from scrap that has been planed down to ½" thickness. You might want to make a few extra wedges because some will fit better than others.

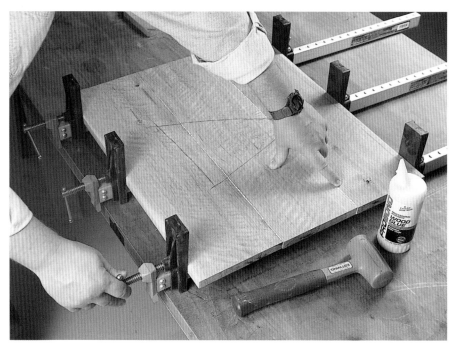

1 After deciding the best arrangement for the boards, apply glue to the edges and clamp the top until all excess squeezes out. Use a hammer and a block to coax mating pieces flush. The three boards for this particular top were arranged to get rid of the knot on one of the boards. That knot, which you can see in the bottom right-hand corner of the top, was eventually cut away as waste. After clamping the top, set it aside for the glue to dry.

Cutouts

Cut the curved cutouts on the bottom of the legs with a jigsaw and clean them up with a spindle sander. If you have decided to have an octagonal top, you might consider making these cutouts as half octagons.

Start the Stretchers

The top and bottom stretchers are joined with a half-lap joint we made with a dado set. After you make your cuts, you'll probably have to clean up your work with a file or shoulder plane to get a good fit.

Stretcher Shoulders

The patterns for the shoulders are on page 55. The top stretcher should measure, shoulder edge to shoulder edge at its widest point, 13¼". The bottom stretcher is 16¾". One thing to keep in mind here is that the shoulders on the stretchers must be beveled or angled at the same angle you beveled your mortises and the tops and bottoms of the legs. We used a band saw for these cuts and cleaned out the waste with a rasp and a file.

Mortises for the Wedges

The location of the ½" × ⅝" mortises on the stretchers are on page 55. The reason these mortises are a little longer than they are wide is to give your wedges something to grab on to. The extra ⅛" in length should be located behind the line where the front face of the leg meets the tenon. This will make for a much tighter joint. Cut the wedges from scrap using the pattern in the plans. Bevel the edges using sandpaper or a belt sander.

Because the table is held together with eight wedges and four screws, make sure all of the mortises and tenons fit snugly. A file and sandpaper will make most of your joints snug. When everything fits well, number your pieces on the insides of the mortises and then finish the disassembled pieces. We used brown aniline dye on the raw wood, then sprayed on a coat of lacquer. When that had dried, we applied a warm brown glaze on all the pieces and wiped the excess glaze away until all the pieces were a uniform color. After allowing the glaze to dry overnight, we applied three more coats

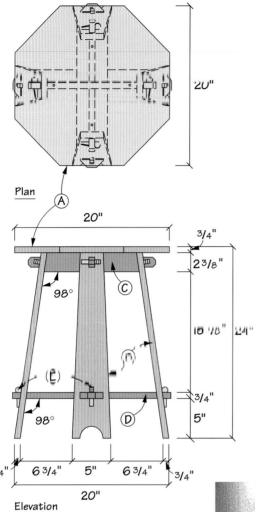

Plan

(A)

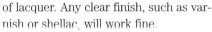

20"

20"

3/4"

2 3/8"

98°

(C)

16 1/8" 24"

(E)

(D)

98°

3/4"

3/4"   6 3/4"   5"   6 3/4"   3/4"

20"

Elevation

Schedule of Materials: Octagonal Taboret

No.	Ltr.	Item	Dimensions T W L	Material
1	A	Top	3/4" x 20" x 20"	White Oak
4	B	Legs	3/4" x 5" x 23 5/8"	White Oak
2	C	Top stretch*	3/4" x 2 3/8" x 16 1/2"	White Oak
2	D	Bot. stretch"	3/4" x 4" x 20 1/2"	White Oak
8	E	Wedges	1/2" x 3/4" x 2 1/2"	White Oak

* These lengths are for the octagonal ends on the stretchers; for the rounded stretchers, add 1 1/4" to the length of the top stretcher and subtract 1/2" from the bottom stretchers.

2 To chain-drill your mortises, set the table on your drill press to 8 degrees and clamp a fence to one end. We used a 3/4" brad-point bit, but you can also use a Forstner or spade bit for this job. Drill from the face of the legs so that any tear-out will occur on the back side, or even better, use a backing board.

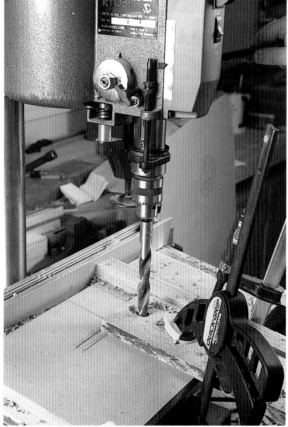

3 After marking the location of the top mortise on the leg, we then marked on the drill table where the board sits when the first hole is drilled and then where it sits when the last hole is made. These marks help you cut the other legs faster and more accurately.

of lacquer. Any clear finish, such as varnish or shellac, will work fine.

When your finish is dry, it's time for the final assembly. First, drill four clearance holes through the top stretchers that will take a 3" screw. Drill or ream these holes into an oval shape to account for future wood movement. Then countersink the holes from the bottom to allow the screw to seat at least 1/2" into the top. Put the base together with the wedges. You might have to use a mallet to get the wedges in snugly. Then put your top facedown on a smooth cloth. Position the base upside down over the center of the top and mark the locations of the four holes on the top. Pilot-drill small holes in the top and then screw your top to the base.

4 *The hardest part about removing the waste is making sure you follow the 8-degree angle you just chain-drilled in the legs. When you're working on the side of the leg that will face out, work the bottom edges and sides of the mortises. Then flip the piece over and clean up the top edges and sides of the mortises.*

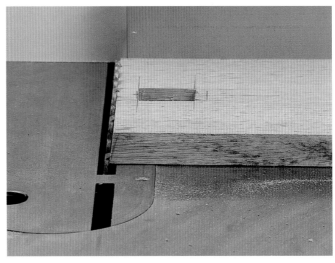

5 *Set your table saw's blade to an 8-degree angle. Cut the bevel on the top of the leg with the front face of the leg facing up. Then turn the piece over so the back side of the leg is facing up, and cut the bevels on the bottom of the legs. Take care not to remove too much material.*

6 *The legs are 5" wide at their base and 3" wide at the top. After marking the line on the leg, cut the taper on your band saw or table saw. Save the scraps to make the wedges for the tenons (or for a doorstop in your shop).*

7 *We used a 3" diameter for the half-circle cutouts. Set your compass to mark a 1½" radius, then put the pin of the compass in the center of each leg at the bottom. Clean the cut with a spindle sander.*

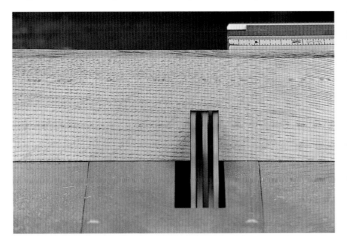

8 *The half-lap joints in the top stretchers were cut with our dado set configured to make a ¾"-wide cut that was 1³⁄₁₆" high (left). The dadoes for the half-lap joints in the bottom stretchers were cut using several passes with a dado that was set for ³⁄₈" high. We made the first and last cuts on the 4"-wide dado (right) and then made several passes to clean out the waste between.*

9 *The shoulders for the tenons on the bottom stretchers must be cut with an 8-degree bevel. Set this angle on your band saw table and make the cuts as shown in the photo (left). Then set your table back to level to cut the shoulders on the top stretchers (right), angling the miter gauge to match. Then make the cuts in from the ends of the stretchers using a fence on your band saw. You won't be able to remove all of the waste this way on the bottom stretchers because of the bevel. So finish those cuts with a backsaw.*

Arts and Crafts Taboret

Full-size diagram of lower
stretcher on taboret

hole for wedge

Line of tenon
shoulder

Profile

Hole for
wedge

Full-size diagram of upper
stretcher on taboret

Full-size diagram of wedge for
the tenons on the taboret

Plan

Stickley Side Table

THIS STICKLEY SIDE TABLE is patterned after the model #562 taboret shown in the L. & J.G. Stickley catalog of 1914. The original of this table now sells for $3,000 or more.

As with all white oak Arts and Crafts pieces, wood figure is important to make a simple design stand out. Choose the best figure for the top and the panel pieces. If the stretchers and legs are also well figured, so much the better.

After cutting the legs to size, mark the best faces for showing off the grain. Then cut ⅜" × 2⅜" × 1" mortises in the legs for the stretchers, and ⅜" × 1⅛" × 1" mortises for the aprons. These mortises are centered on the width of the legs and located as shown in the diagram. I used a benchtop mortiser for this step, but you could also use a plunge router with an up-spiral bit to cut them.

Now change the bit (either mortiser or router bit) to a ¼" bit and mark and cut the ¼" × ⅝" × ⅝" mortises for the panels in the aprons and stretchers.

With the mortises complete, head for the table saw and get ready to cut tenons. I use a rip blade to form my tenons. I cut the cheeks first, then define the shoulders, so there isn't a chance of the shoulders being accidentally notched by the saw blade during the cheek cut. By cutting the shoulder last, any "notching" will happen against the tenon cheek.

When making the shoulder cut on the table saw, it's easiest to use the rip fence to define the 1" tenon length. If you use the fence to the right of the blade, and the miter gauge to the left of the blade, you will trap the fall-off piece between the blade and fence, causing it to shoot back from the blade. Instead set the fence for 10" to the right of the blade and use the miter gauge to the right of the blade, as well. This way you can cut both tenoned ends with a single setup, and the waste will fall harmlessly to the left of the blade.

If you're paying careful attention, you will realize 1" tenons are going to bump into one another in the mortises. After cutting the tenon shoulders, reset the fence and the blade angle to cut 45-degree miters on the ends of the tenons.

Don't leave the saw yet. You still need to form the ¼" × 5¼" × ½" tenons on both ends of the panels. You might have noticed that the tenons are ⅛" less wide than the mortise dimensions. This is no mistake. When the side panels are positioned between the stretchers and aprons, the shoulders of the panel tenons will fit snugly against the stretchers and rails. If the mortises in the legs were the exact width of the tenons, and off by even a little bit, they would force a gap between the panels and the two rails. The ⅛" extra space on the panel tenons is to allow for wood movement.

Next, mark the 1" curve on the bottom edge of each stretcher and cut the shape on the band saw. The easiest way to mark this curve is with a flexible ⅛" wood strip bent to the 1" mark and then traced with a pencil.

One last step before assembly. The top is held in place by tabletop fasteners. These are screwed into the underside of the top, and fit into ⅛"-wide grooves in the aprons. These fasteners allow the top to adjust to wood movement without affecting the base. Run these grooves on all four aprons on the table saw. This will let you decide which way the top will fit later.

You're ready to sand, then glue up the base. A dry fit is definitely a good idea to make sure everything fits and to make sure you know how to hold everything in place once the glue goes on.

With the base glued and clamped, cut the pieces for the top and glue them together. To reduce the amount of sanding necessary, a few biscuits added to the joint will help align the pieces and keep them from slipping during glue-up.

When the base is ready, mark each of the peg locations on the mortise-and-tenon joints, and drill a 1¼" × ¼" hole at each location. Then peg the holes with ¼" oak dowels. Cut the excess dowel length flush to the table leg and finish sand.

Unclamp the top and sand it flat. Then mark 2½" in from each corner and run a line at a 45-degree angle to clip the corners of the top on the band saw

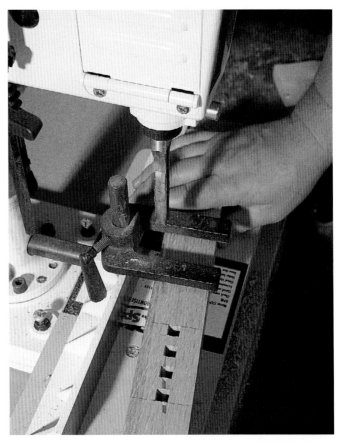

The best method for mortising is to first bore the areas at either end of the mortise, then space the next few mortises the width of the mortising chisel. In this case, the spacing works almost perfectly. The goal is to allow the chisel bit to have enough wood to drill straight without wandering from side to side. On some mortises the spacing between the first holes will be less than the width of the chisel (left). Complete the mortise by drilling away the waste between the first mortises. This allows the mortise chisel to cut most efficiently without pulling to the left or right and bending the chisel (right).

to an octagonal shape. Then finish sand the top.

I used the same finish on the table that was used on the Morris chair. If you've built the chair, as well, put a nice lamp on the table, get a good book, and sit down to some early 20th-century comfort.

Schedule of Materials: Stickley Side Table

No.	Item	Dimensions T W L	Material	Comments
4	Legs	2" x 2" x 21⅞"	WO	
4	Stretchers	⅞" x 3" x 14"	WO	1" TBE
4	Aprons	⅞" x 1 ½" x 14"	WO	1" TBE
4	Panels	½" x 6" x 8½"	WO	½" TBE
1	Top	⅞" x 20" x 20"	WO	
16	Pegs	¼" x 1 ½"	Oak	Dowel stock

WO = white oak
TBE = tenon on both ends

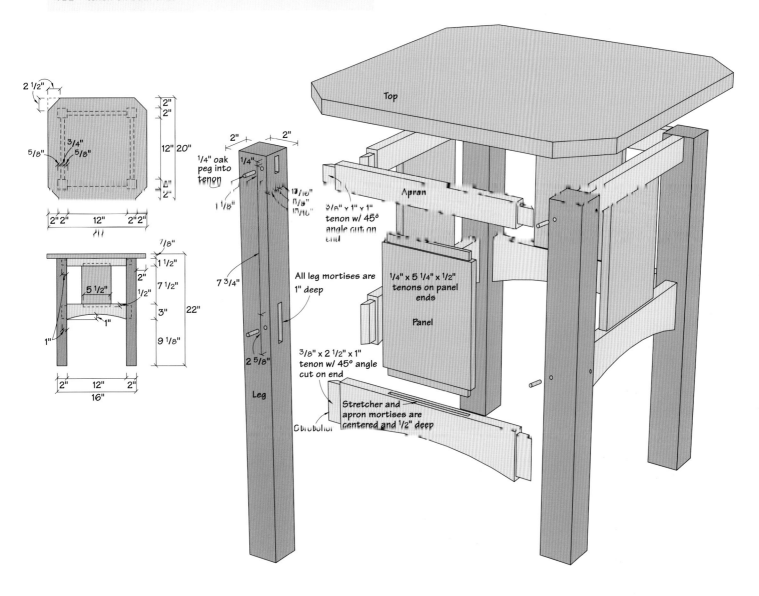

Show off your pottery, books and good taste with this
authentic reproduction of a turn-of-the-century classic.

Limbert Two-Door Bookcase

IN 1996, I STOPPED PURCHASING ARTS AND CRAFTS FURNITURE, and this bookcase is the reason why. After collecting Arts and Crafts furniture since 1990, I had amassed a small but nice collection on my salary as a newspaper reporter. However, the piece I wanted but never could find was a glass-front bookcase. So I patiently saved my money and went to an auction in Chicago, ready to buy this very bookcase, which had been featured prominently in the auction's catalog.

I was outbid. Completely blown out of the water is more like it. I went home that day with two smaller pieces that, while nice, were not exactly what I wanted. So like any scorned woodworker, I plotted and planned. I sought out dimensions from auction catalogs and reprints of historical materials. And then I built the bookcase I'd always wanted. Limbert pieces were almost always made from quarter-sawn oak or ash, but I decided that cherry with a deep mahogany finish was what I wanted.

Everything about this piece is as authentic as I could get, from the knob to the shiplapped beadboard back. My only compromises were some nonmortise hinges (I'm convinced Limbert would have used these if Amerock had been making them in 1904), and a thin bead of silicone to help hold the glass in place. Construction is simple — well within the reach of most beginning and intermediate woodworkers. The top, bottom and gallery back rest in dadoes

in the sides. The beadboard back is screwed into a rabbet on the back. And the doors are simple mortise and tenon construction. In fact, the only tricky part is the mullions and muntins on the doors. But if you take some care when building them, you should have no problem at all.

You need about 60 board feet of 4/4 cherry to build the Limbert two-door bookcase, and not a scrap of plywood. Begin by surfacing all your material and gluing up any panels you might needs for the sides, top, bottom or shelves.

Start With the Sides

Begin working on the case by cutting the ⅜" × ⅝" rabbets on the back edges of the top, bottom and side pieces for the back. The rabbeting bit I own for my router table wasn't large enough to make this cut easily, so I made the rabbet in two passes on the table saw. While you're at the saw, make the shallow ⅛" × ⅜" rabbet on the ends of the gallery back. This rabbet allows the gallery back to lock into the rabbet on the side pieces.

Now it's time to mill the ⅜"-deep dadoes on the sides that will hold the top and bottom in place. Make a simple plywood jig (it takes about five minutes) to cut these dadoes. First study Photo 1 to see generally what the jig looks like. Basically it's two pieces of plywood with two pieces of scrap nailed to them. You'll notice that the two pieces of plywood that the router rides on are differ-

ent widths. This is no mistake. One of them is 4" wide and the other is 2" wide. The dado that holds the top needs to go 4" from the top edge. The dado that holds the bottom needs to go 2" from the bottom edge. With this little jig, all you need to do to make a perfectly placed dado is put the 4"-wide part flush against the top edge of the side. Clamp the jig in place, and make the dado cut using a pattern bit chucked into your plunge router. Turn the jig around and put the 2"-wide edge against the bottom edge and cut the dado for the bottom.

Here's the easy way to make the jig: Rip the two pieces of plywood to size and place them on top of one of the side pieces. Now put pieces of ¾"-thick scrap under the plywood that's the same thickness as the sides. Now take another piece of scrap that's exactly as thick as your top and bottom pieces and place it between the two pieces of plywood.

Press the pieces of plywood together against the piece of scrap between them and nail the plywood to the wood below. Your jig is done.

Place the jig on top of the sides, clamp it down and rout the ¾"-wide by ⅜"-deep dadoes for the top and sides. You'll need to make these dadoes in at least two passes.

Before you can assemble the case, you need to cut the ½" radius on the front corner of the side pieces and the front corners of the top piece, which extends beyond the front of the case by ¼". Make the pattern using a piece of plywood. Cut the radius on the plywood using a band saw and then sand it smooth. Use this pattern with a pattern-cutting bit in your router to shape the corners.

Now sand all the case parts up to 150-grit and get ready to assemble the case.

Assembly

To assemble the case, I recommend you use polyurethane glue. First, it is superior to yellow glue for joining long grain to end grain. Second, it has a long open time so you have about 40 minutes to make sure your cabinet is square.

If you've never used polyurethane glue, let me tell you that you should use as little as possible because the foamy squeeze-out is no fun to clean up. I like to coat one part that's being glued with a very thin (but consistent) film of the glue.

Then I wipe a little water on the part it's being joined to. Water activates the glue and speeds curing. Glue the top, bottom and gallery back between the sides. Clamp up your case and let it sit overnight.

When the glue has cured, take the case out of the clamps and drill the holes for your adjustable shelf pins. I made a plywood jig using my drill press and a 5mm bit. I drilled holes every 3" and placed each row 2" from the front and back of the cabinet. Finally, glue the kick to the bottom of the case. I used biscuits to keep the piece aligned as I clamped it to the bottom.

The Back

If you've never built a solid wood shiplapped back, I think you're going to find the reward is well worth the effort. Build the back before you build the doors because the back, when screwed in place, holds your case square. This is critical when hanging your doors.

Make your back pieces out of any scrap pieces of cherry you might have lying around. Thin pieces are OK. You just want to make sure that the width of the pieces will add up to 31¼" when

1 *This plywood jig cuts the dadoes in the sides that hold the top and bottom pieces. Here I'm cutting the dado for the bottom. Note how the edge of the jig is flush to the bottom of the case.*

Schedule of Materials: Limbert Two-Door Bookcase

CABINET

No.	Ltr.	Item	Dimensions T W L	Comments
2	A	Sides	¾" x 12" x 46"	½"
1	B	Top	¾" x 12¼" x 31¼"	in ⅜" dado
1	C	Bottom	¾" x 12" x 31¼"	in ⅜" dado
1	D	Gallery back	¾" x 4" x 31¼"	in ⅜" x ⅝" rabbet
1	E	Kick	¾" x 2" x 30½"	
2	F	Adj. shelves	¾" x 10½" x 30⅜"	
	G	Back	⅝" x 31¼" x 38¾"	in ⅜" x ⅝" rabbet

DOORS

No.	Ltr.	Item	Dimensions T W L	Comments
4	H	Stiles	¾" x 1¾" x 38"	
2	I	Top rails	¾" x 1¾" x 13¾"	1" TBE
2	J	Mid. rails	¾" x 1" x 13¾"	1" TBE
2	K	Bot. rails	¾" x 2" x 13¾"	1" TBE
2	L	Mid. stiles	¾" x 1" x 13"	½" TBE
		Retaining strips	¼" x ¼"	

TBE= tenon on both ends

placed in the rabbet in the case sides.

Begin by cutting ⁵⁄₁₆"-deep by ¼"-wide rabbets on the edges. I like to use a rabbeting bit in a router table. Cut the rabbet on both long edges of the boards for the back — except the boards that will go on either end. Those need the rabbet on only one edge. Now cut the bead on one edge of the back pieces using a beading bit in your router table. Beading bits look confusing at first. Just remember to run the boards on edge through your router table.

Now fit your back pieces in place in the rabbet in the case. Put quarters between your back boards to space out the boards. This allows the back to expand and contract with the seasons (Photo 2). When everything fits, screw the back boards in place. Use only two screws to attach the back boards: one at the top and one at the bottom. (This will prevent your back from self-destructing later.) On the boards on the end you can also screw the back boards into the side pieces.

Doors

I like to build my doors to the exact size of the opening and then cut them down to size on the jointer. These doors are built using mortise-and-tenon construction. I cut my tenons on a table saw using a dado stack and then used them to lay out my mortises.

All the tenons for the doors are ⅜" thick. The tenons on the rails are all 1" long. The tenons on the middle stiles are ½" long. I cut ¼" shoulders on all the tenons.

When cutting your mortises, make them ¹⁄₁₆" deeper than the tenon is long. This prevents your tenon from bottoming out in your mortise.

Check the fit of everything and then glue up the doors. When the glue is dry, you need to cut ⅜" × ⅜" rabbets on the back side of the door to hold the glass. The best way to do this is to use a bearing-guided rabbeting bit in your router table as shown (Photo 3).

Take it slow in the corners so you don't blow out the wood around the middle stile and middle rail. Sand your doors and get ready to hang them.

2 *Get a pocketful of quarters when putting the back in place. You want the back to expand and contract with the seasons and the thickness of a quarter is just about right.*

Dealing With Warped Doors

Once you hang your doors, you might find that the stiles don't line up just right. No matter how flat you plane your stock, there's still a chance that your stiles won't be perfect and one will bend out in front of the other.

There are two ways of dealing with this. First, you can make your door parts out of two thin pieces of cherry laminated together. I made these stiles from two pieces of ½" cherry that I glued together at the face and then planed the lamination down to ¾".

This process produces a primitive form of two-ply plywood that will resist warping.

Second, after you hang your doors, you can cheat by removing the warp with a hand plane. With the doors hung in the case, mark the one that sticks out. Use a pencil to draw a line on the edge of this proud door all along the place where it juts forth.

Take the door off its hinges and plane the stile down to that line using a hand plane. Re-hang the door and check your work.

Get a Perfect Gap

The goal when hanging an inset door like this is to get a ¹⁄₁₆" gap all around. If your case is square and your doors are square, it's going to be a simple task.

Start by putting one of the doors in place and hold the stile against the side. This is where you're going to find out if everything is square. If things are square, you can just start shaving off a

little bit from the stiles and rails until you have the gap you want.

If things aren't square, you need to make some tapered cuts on your doors. You can do this on your jointer, but I prefer to use a hand plane to shave off the excess. This allows you to stop your cut exactly where you want it. Keep working at it until the gap looks reasonably uniform.

Now hang the doors. I use Amerock nonmortise hinges. These hinges are adjustable so you can get your inset doors lined up just right. And installing them is a snap.

First screw the hinges to the case. Then attach the doors to the hinges using spring clamps. Drill pilot holes for your screws and screw the doors to the hinges. Remove the spring clamps. While you're at it, add the knob and the catches you've chosen to hold the doors shut.

Remove all the hardware and then cut some ¼" × ¼" strips to hold the glass in place. Sand everything to 150-grit and prepare for finishing.

Finishing

This finish consists of a reddish dye, followed by a coat of lacquer, a coat of warm brown glaze and then three more coats of lacquer. Begin the finishing with a water-based dye. I use Moser's Light Sheraton Mahogany dye. Then I covered the entire project with one coat of Lilly's warm brown glaze. You can usually find glaze at professional paint stores for about $26 a gallon. Wipe the

SUPPLIES

4 - Amerock nonmortise hinges
Woodworkers Supply
(800) 645-9292
Item # 890626 • $2.95 each

1 - Moser's Light Sheraton
Mahogany dye
Item # 844414 • $11.90 each

2 - 1¹⁵⁄₁₆" double catch
Lee Valley Tools
(800) 871-8158 or
www.leevalley.com

2 - 1¹⁵⁄₁₆" double catch
Item # 00W12.02 • $1.40 each

1 - Brass knob
Item # 01A21.24 • $2.40 each

2 - Bronze shelving sleeves (20)
Item # 63Z05.03 • $2.95 each

1 - Bronze shelving supports (20)
Item # 63Z05.04 • $2.95 each

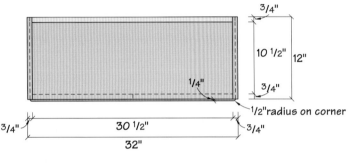

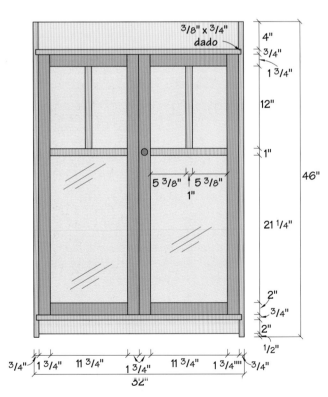

Elevation

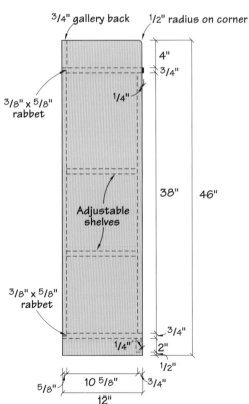

Profile

3 *Cut the rabbet for the glass using a rabbeting bit in your router table. After the rabbet is cut, you'll need to square the edges with a chisel. Because this work is delicate, make sure your chisel is extra sharp.*

glaze on with a cheesecloth. Allow it to flash after a couple minutes, and then wipe off the excess until you achieve an even tone. Allow the glaze to dry overnight. Finally, apply three coats of a clear finish.

Glass

Normally I would pin the strips to the doors to hold the glass in place. But because the muntins and mullions are so small this was out of the question. Silicone to the rescue. Put a small bead of 100-percent clear silicone in the rabbet and place the ⅛" glass in place. Then run another small bead of silicone in the gap between the wood and the glass and press the wooden strips in place. Use spring clamps to hold them in place while the silicone sets up (Photo 4).

Now that the bookcase is done, I plan to set it up in my study, right where I always envisioned it. And the first thing I'm going to put in there is all those auction catalogs I don't have any more use for.

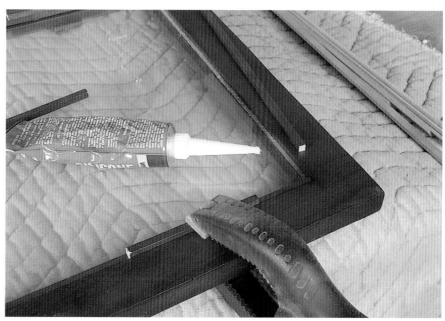

4 *Put down a thin bead of silicone in the rabbet, then put the glass on that. Then lay down another bead of silicone and press the wooden strip into place to cover all the goop. Now your doors look good when both open and shut.*

This turn-of-the-century classic fits in almost any floor plan.

Roycroft Magazine Stand

During the Arts and Crafts heyday at the turn of the 20th century an extraordinary number of designs for bookcase and magazine stands were offered to the public as completed pieces and construction plans. Most included simple designs and straightforward construction. A variation of the design shown here appears in the Dover Publications reprint of the 1906 Roycroft Furniture Catalog from the Roycroft Shop in East Aurora, New York.

Slabs

In keeping with the Arts and Crafts style of stout furniture, the sides and shelves of this piece are called out as ⅞"-thick material. You may find the design more economically feasible by changing that to ¾" material. Start by milling and matching the grain patterns on the two side pieces. If possible, try to use only two boards per side for the width. If this isn't possible, the trapezoidal design will allow you to use two 7"-wide boards for the center of each side, adding a 2" strip on the front and back edges of the lower half, keeping the exposed glue lines to a minimum.

With the sides glued, squared up and sanded flat, mark the location of the shelves as shown on the diagram. The top and bottom shelves will have angled through-mortises cut into the sides, while the other four shelves are captured between the sides in ⅜"-deep stopped dadoes. To mark the start and stop locations of the dadoes, draw the

Who Were the Roycrofters?

The Roycrofter handicraft community was founded in East Aurora, New York in 1894 by Elbert Hubbard. The Arts and Crafts philosophy behind the skillful hand crafting of simple furniture is resonant in the following quote by Hubbard: "One machine can do the work of 50 ordinary men. No machine can do the work of one extraordinary man." The origin of the Roycroft name is debatable, but the explanation most widely given is that the word means 'king's craft,' or the best of a craftsman's work, fit to be given to a king.

Dissatisfied with his career as a soap salesman, Hubbard traveled to England where he met William Morris and was impressed by Morris' Arts and Crafts Kelmscott Press. After returning to the United States, Hubbard launched the Roycroft Press in order to publish his series of biographical sketches, entitled *Little Journeys*.

How does this fit into the history of Art and Crafts furniture? Hubbard became such a famous writer and inspirational speaker that visitors flocked to East Aurora to meet Elbert Hubbard or to live in the Roycroft community. An inn was built to house the large amount of visitors, and Hubbard commissioned local craftsmen to build a simple, straight-lined style of furniture to furnish the inn. A furniture manufacturing company was born when visitors expressed a desire to purchase the furniture. Original Roycroft furniture was massive and heavy, usually produced from oak or mahogany, and known for its severe lines.

The Roycroft community lasted only from 1895 to 1938 (flourishing shortly before Hubbard's death in 1915), but examples of Roycroft bookbinding, metalsmithing and furniture making are still highly sought after today by collectors. Roycroft crafts are sought not only by collectors, but also by anyone who simply appreciates the beauty and craftsmanship of these items. Original Roycroft furniture is hard to find today, but the Roycroft Renaissance movement has caught the attention of furniture makers, resulting in authentic-looking reproductions.

Interested in learning more about the Roycrofters? Charles F. Hamilton's *Roycroft Collectibles* (SPS Publications, 1994) is a must-have book for Roycroft collectors, and Kevin McConnell's *Roycroft Art Metal* (Schiffer Publishing, 1997) will be of specific interest to anyone seeking information about Roycroft metalwork.

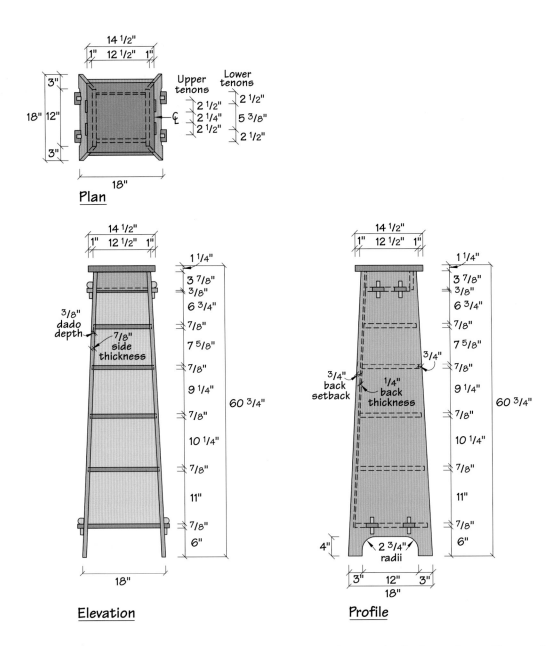

Plan

Elevation

Profile

shape of the sides on the side blanks, then measure in ¾" from the front and back edges.

Cut the dadoes with a plunge router and a router guide. Even though the sides of the stand are angled 3 degrees, the dadoes can be cut at a 90-degree angle to the side, leaving only a slight gap on the underside of each shelf. If you prefer to eliminate the gap, use a wood strip to tilt the router at a 3 degree angle. If you opt for the angled dadoes, run a test piece or you may inadvertently transfer your gap to the top of the shelf.

The through-mortises can also be cut using a router with the base tilted to a

3-degree angle or marked and hand cut. In either case, cut from the outside surface to keep any tear-out to the inside of the case. Use a scrap backing board to reduce the tear-out even further.

Trapezoids and Shelves

With the dadoes and through-mortises complete, crosscut the top and bottom edges of the sides at a 3-degree angle, then use a band saw or a jigsaw and a plane to shape the sides. Next, mark and cut the elongated half oval at the base of each side to form the legs. Lastly, mark the back edge of each side for a ¼"-wide by ⅜" groove for the back. The groove should be set in ¾" from the

back edge and start 6" up on the sides, running through at the top.

Next cut the shelves to size. The four center shelves can be cut to the sizes given in the Schedule of Materials, with all four edges cut on a 3-degree angle. The top and bottom shelves are a little more complicated. Each must have the through-tenons cut to size and shape (see page 70 for a pattern of the tenon), and the end of the shelf should be pared with a chisel on a 3-degree angle to match the inside surface of the sides. Don't cut the mortises for the wedges at this time. See "Wedges" on page 71.

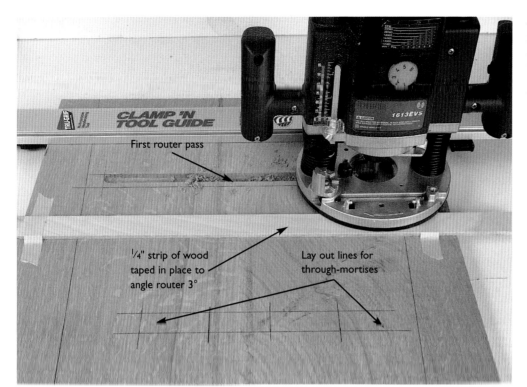

A $1/4$"-thick strip of wood is taped in place on the side slab to give a 3-degree angle to the shelf dadoes and the through-mortises. Using a $1/4$" straight router bit required moving the setup once for each dado to achieve the $7/8$" width necessary.

First router pass

$1/4$" strip of wood taped in place to angle router 3°

Lay out lines for through-mortises

Dry Assemble the Back and Drawer

This next step can be a little awkward, so if you have a friend handy, give him or her a call. Dry assemble the stand by laying one side flat so the through-mortises hang over the edge of the table. Place the shelves in their respective dadoes and insert the through-tenons into the mortises. Then place the other side over the tenons and insert the shelves. To hold everything in place, use soft-jawed clamps across the width of the stand placed underneath the through-tenons. This should pull the tenons and the shelves into place. Check the fit and adjust as necessary.

With the stand still dry assembled, measure for the trapezoidal back, allowing as tight a fit in the back grooves as possible. The bottom of the back will overlay the back edge of the bottom shelf and be tacked in place to the shelf. The top of the back should be flush to the top of the sides.

With the stand still dry assembled, mark the location of the sides on the top and bottom surfaces of the shelf tenons extending through the sides. Then disassemble the stand and drill out or hand cut through-mortises through each tenon to accept the

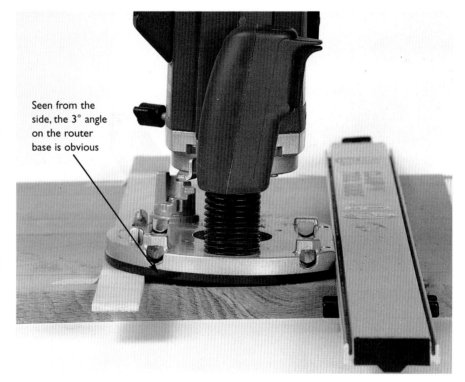

Seen from the side, the 3° angle on the router base is obvious

The upper mortise has been drilled out with a Forstner bit, while the lower one has been drilled, then squared with a chisel

A jigsaw was used to roughout the shape of the base

Taper the sides only after completing all the necessary milling in the sides. I used a jigsaw to cut the sides to size, then smoothed up the edges with a bench plane.

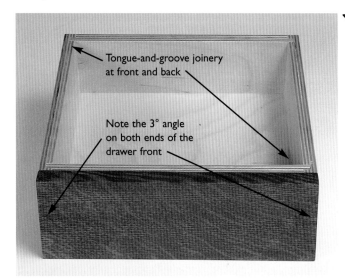

Tongue-and-groove joinery at front and back

Note the 3° angle on both ends of the drawer front

The drawer is made of ¹⁄₂" Baltic birch plywood, and it uses tongue-and-groove construction. A more complex joint could have been used, but the drawer is unlikely to see any heavy use and could be left out altogether.

Schedule of Materials: Roycroft Magazine Stand

No.	Item	Dimensions T W L	Material
1	Top	$1\frac{1}{4}$" x $14\frac{1}{2}$" x $14\frac{1}{2}$"	White oak
2	Sides	$\frac{7}{8}$" x 18" x $59\frac{1}{2}$"	White oak
1	Bottom shelf	$\frac{7}{8}$" x $15\frac{9}{16}$" x 20"	White oak
1	Shelf	$\frac{7}{8}$" x $14\frac{5}{16}$" x $15\frac{7}{16}$"	White oak
1	Shelf	$\frac{7}{8}$" x $13\frac{3}{16}$" x $14\frac{3}{8}$"	White oak
1	Shelf	$\frac{7}{8}$" x $12\frac{1}{8}$" x $13\frac{7}{16}$"	White oak
1	Shelf	$\frac{7}{8}$" x $11\frac{1}{4}$" x $12\frac{11}{16}$"	White oak
1	Top shelf	$\frac{7}{8}$" x $9\frac{1}{2}$" x $15\frac{5}{16}$"	White oak
8	Wedges	$\frac{3}{4}$" x $1\frac{1}{4}$" x $3\frac{1}{2}$"	White oak
1	Back	$\frac{1}{4}$" x 16" x $53\frac{1}{2}$"	Oak plywood
1	Drwr. front	$\frac{3}{4}$" x $3\frac{7}{8}$" x $10\frac{9}{16}$"	White oak
2	Drwr. sides	$\frac{3}{4}$" x 3" x 8"	Birch plywood
2	Drwr. ends	$\frac{3}{4}$" x 3" x $9\frac{1}{4}$"	Birch plywood
1	Drwr. bottom	$\frac{1}{4}$" x $7\frac{1}{2}$" x $9\frac{1}{4}$"	Birch plywood

Magazine Stand

Full-size diagram of mortise, tenon and tusk.

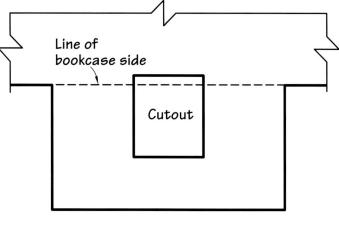

Line of bookcase side

Cutout

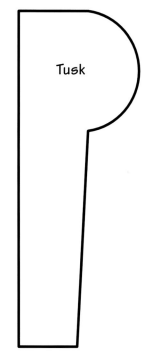

Tusk

wedges. Note that the inside edge of the mortise should be ⅛" or so inside your marks to allow the wedges to draw the stand up tight. The diagram shows how the joint works, and the plans on page 70 offer a pattern for the wedge itself. Cut the wedges a little oversized, reassemble the stand and fit the wedges in place. Make sure you mark the wedges so you'll be able to reassemble the piece easily.

If you haven't noticed, this stand includes a little drawer just below the top. While not of a size to store a great many things, it's a good place for hiding an extra set of keys. The drawer itself is of simple box construction using tongue-and-groove joinery with a bottom captured in a groove. The angled

sides of the stand serve as indexing runners to keep the drawer centered left to right. The drawer face is cut to match the shape of the sides and over hangs the top shelf, which serves as a drawer stop. Screw the face to the drawer box from the inside.

Topping Things Off

The top is a simple slab of wood that is attached to the sides by dowels. I carefully drilled dowel locations in the tops of the assembled sides. I then used dowel centers placed in the holes to locate the mating locations on the underside of the top piece.

With the top fit, disassemble the stand again and sand all the pieces through 220-grit. To finish the piece, I

first applied a coat of brown mahogany gel stain. When the stain was dry, I applied a coat of clear lacquer, sanded and then applied a coat of warm brown glaze. After the glaze had dried overnight, I added two more coats of lacquer.

Assemble the stand as you did during the dry fit, tapping the wedges in place to hold the stand tightly together. If you plan on ever disassembling the piece, use a couple of screws to attach the back to the lower shelf and to the two center shelves for support. Then slip the top into place over the dowels. If you won't be disassembling the piece, use brads to attach the back and add some glue to the dowels to secure the top.

Wedges

The wedged through mortises are the joints that hold the whole stand together. The diagram at right gives the details of how they should look when completed. The mortises are chopped through the tenons with a chisel, but to make things a little more complicated, they should be hand cut on a 3-degree angle to follow the angle of the sides. The tusks are cut on the band saw to the dimensions shown on page 70, but should be left a little oversized until they can be test fit.

In the old days different manufacturers used different styles of wedges. It's one of the ways collectors can quickly identify a piece. Some made the wedges with a round top. Others used half an octagon. A few even carved the wedges, which gives the piece a more medieval look.

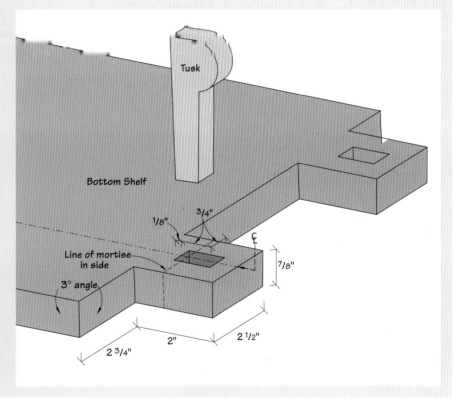

Designed to travel, this slant-sided bookcase was the perfect early-1900s answer to buying furniture through the mail.

Knockdown Bookcase

THE ARTS AND CRAFTS FURNITURE MOVEMENT was also part of another in-~~teresting social change in America~~ the advent of mail-order purchases. ~~Catalogs from Sears and Montgomery Ward were all the rage, and many com-~~ panies took their cue and offered their wares for sale through catalogs rather than set up expensive retail establishments throughout the country. While a great idea in many respects, it raised a difficult problem with furniture. The majority of space in any piece of furniture is air. While air is very light, it's also bulky, and expensive to ship. So furniture makers perfected a style of furniture that continues today — knockdown furniture. Finished disassembled, the furniture could be shipped flat, then simply assembled by the owner. Through-tenons with tusks were the turn-of-the-20th-century answer, while hidden cam-locking hardware is the answer today.

Slanted Construction

This project is actually a very simple bookcase made challenging by slanting the sides. Many of the knockdown bookcases had straight sides, but why do things the easy way? Another slant-side piece in this book (Roycroft magazine stand) also offers the challenge of slanted sides, and is also a piece I did. You will notice the method of making the sides slant is different in each project, and you may want to consider which way appeals to you most.

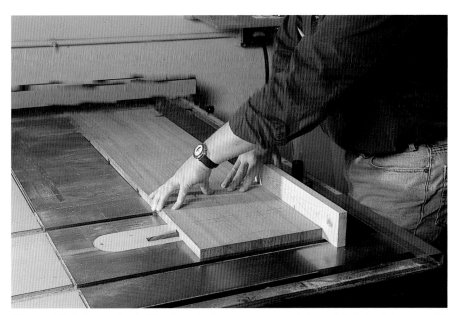

After carefully laying out the shelf locations, the sides are run over a dado stack (set at a 5-degree angle) using the saw's miter gauge to support the side on the final cuts.

Start construction by preparing the blanks for the sides and four shelves. If you aren't fortunate enough to have pieces wide enough to make single-board pieces, glue up the shelves or sides, but make sure you orient your joint so that it will fall in the center of the finished piece. This is less important on the shelves, but since the sides come to a peak at the center the joint becomes obvious if you're off the mark. Also, you can cut the top and bottom shelves to length, but leave the center two shelves long at this time. When the through-tenons are cut and fit you can measure for the exact length of the center shelves.

Critical Pencil Lines

With the blanks prepared, take one of the sides and lay out the shelf locations, mortise locations and the overall shape in pencil on the side. To allow you to do a minimum of angled or beveled cutting on the pieces, the shelves all fit into ¾"-wide by ⅜"-deep dadoes cut at a 5-degree angle in the sides using the table saw. Because of this, the location of the shelves actually falls at an angle on the sides. A ¹⁄₁₆" difference in shelf height one way or the other won't dramatically affect the use of the bookcase, but you must make sure that the dadoes are cut at the same locations on each side.

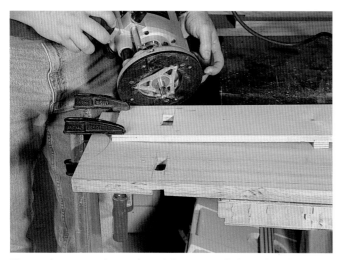

This simple scrap-wood jig made angled mortises a fairly simple task.

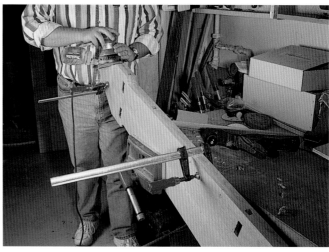

With the sides clamped together and mounted in my vice, shaping the sides took some sanding and planing.

If you happen to have a sliding table on your table saw, you're in great shape. Most people don't, so the next best option to cut the angled dadoes is to use your miter gauge. If you don't already have a substantial wooden fence attached to your gauge, now is a good time. A fence that is 18" to 24" long and about 3" high will work fine. You will need to determine which way to orient the sides on your saw depending on the way the arbor of your saw tilts. With some of the cuts, the majority of the side will be supported by the miter gauge, and you can safely use your rip fence to guide your cut. When the larger section of the side will be between the blade and rip fence, this is an unsafe cut. The board can twist and bind against the blade causing kickback. Move the rip fence out of the way, carefully mark the sides and make the next cuts with only the miter gauge fence. With the dadoes complete, change the dado to a crosscut blade, and bevel the bottom edge of each side.

Through-Mortising at an Angle
The next step is the through-mortises. For these to work correctly they also need to be cut at a 5-degree angle, and they must fall directly in the dadoes you just cut on the saw. You could cut them by hand, but the 5-degree angle is tricky to maintain. You could also set up a mortiser as I did in the other stand, but I got a little smarter this time and

came up with a router template.

By using a piece of ½" Baltic birch with a strip added to its back, I was able to make a router template guide that would make cuts at a 5-degree angle. It takes some rearranging of the guide for the different cuts, but the results work rather well. Again, careful layout lines are critical here. To make a 5-degree ramp, I used a scrap piece of ½" material for the back strip, nailed to the template 14" from the end. Check this dimension on your materials to get as close to 5 degrees as possible.

The rest is fairly simple. Check the offset on your router template guide from the bit, and add this to the ¾" × 2" dimension for the mortise. Mark that size on the template and use a drill and jigsaw or scroll saw to make a clean, square hole in your template.

Clamp the template in place over the mortise locations and cut your through-mortises using two or three depth settings. Depending on the router bit you are using, you may want to use a backing board behind the side to reduce tear-out. I used a jigsaw to square up most of the mortises, and finished the job with a sharp chisel.

Shaping up the Sides
The next step is to cut the sides to their "spade" shape. I used my band saw for most of this work, but used a jigsaw to cut the radii under the top shelf and the arch at the bottom. Cut a

little wide of your layout lines, then clamp the sides together, aligning the sides by the shelf grooves on the inside surface. Plane and sand the sides to matching shapes.

Fitting the Through-Tenons
Now it's time to start to fit things together. Start by checking the fit of your shelves in the dadoes in the sides. Mine were a hair thick, so I was able to run them down on the planer to make an almost perfect fit. Check the width of the bottom shelf against the width of the sides at the shelf location, now that the sides are shaped. Adjust the shelf as necessary. Next, fit the shelf into the dado, and from the outside, mark the tenon location through the mortise on the end of the shelf. Remove the shelf and mark off the 2" length of each mortise, then head for the band saw again. The width of the tenons is the critical cut. The shoulder of the tenons shouldn't be too messed up, but that edge is buried in the side's dadoes, so it doesn't have to be perfect.

With the bottom shelf tenons cut, start fitting the shelf and sides together. You want a snug fit, but not too loose and not too tight. A chisel, file or rasp and some sanding should do the job. Take your time and get it right.

With the bottom shelf fit, check the dimensions on the top shelf, mark the tenons and repeat the fitting process. When that task is complete, you can fit

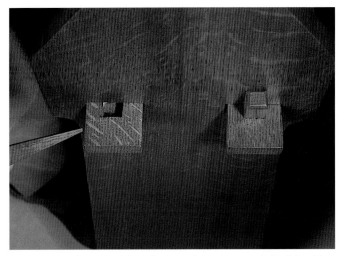

A close look at the wedged through-tenons shows the recess behind the side that allows the wedge to pull the sides tight.

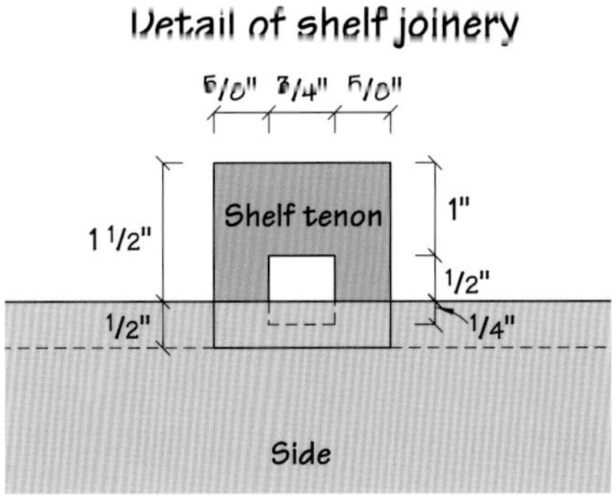

the two center shelves and slide them into position. These shelves are designed to be left loose, but if they slide a little more than you like, a single nail through the side into the center of the shelf will make a permanent solution, or you can drive a short piece of wedge into the joint under the shelf for a temporary fix.

Tusks and the Home Stretch

To hold the top and bottom shelves in place — and the whole case together — disassemble the case and mark the ¾" × ¾" through-mortises on the shelf tenons as shown in the diagrams. I used my mortising machine to cut these holes, but a drill press would also work, with a chisel to square out the corners.

Reassemble the case, then cut the eight tusks as shown in the diagrams. Appropriately, the tusks should seat with their center at the shelf tenon. Fit the tusks as necessary, and tap them into place to make the whole case rigid. Now take it all apart one last time and sand everything to 150-grit.

For a finish, I used a simple dark-colored gel stain, wiping off the excess till I was happy with the depth of the color. I then top-coated the case with a couple of coats of lacquer.

The nicest thing about moving this bookcase is that by knocking out the eight tusks, everything fits in the trunk of a compact car.

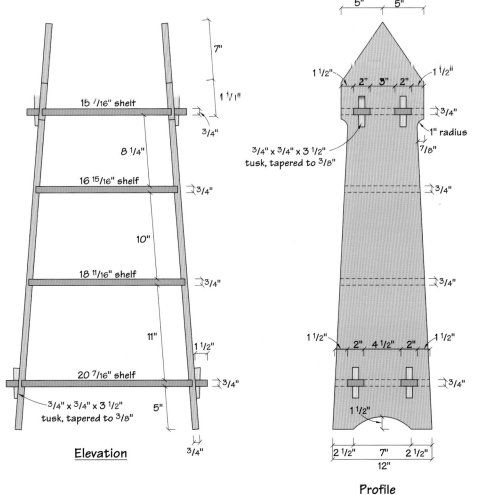

Detail of shelf joinery

5/8"   3/4"   5/8"

Shelf tenon

1 1/2"   1"   1/2"   1/4"

1/2"

Side

Elevation

7"   1 1/4"   3/4"

15 7/16" shelf

8 1/4"

16 15/16" shelf   3/4"

10"

18 11/16" shelf   3/4"

11"   1 1/2"

20 7/16" shelf   3/4"

3/4" x 3/4" x 3 1/2" tusk, tapered to 3/8"   5"

3/4"

Profile

5"   5"

1 1/2"   2"   3"   2"   1 1/2"

3/4"

1" radius

7/8"

3/4" x 3/4" x 3 1/2" tusk, tapered to 3/8"

3/4"

3/4"

1 1/2"   2"   4 1/2"   2"   1 1/2"

3/4"

1 1/2"

2 1/2"   7"   2 1/2"
12"

Schedule of Materials: Knockdown Bookcase

No.	Item	Dimensions T W L	Material
2	Sides	¾" × 12" × 48"	White oak
1	Bottom shelf	¾" × 11⅛" × 24½"	White oak
1	Top shelf	¾" × 10" × 19½"	White oak
1	Third shelf	¾" × 9⅞" × 18¹¹⁄₁₆"	White oak
1	Second shelf	¾" × 8¹¹⁄₁₆" × 16¹⁵⁄₁₆"	White oak
8	Tusks	¾" × ¾" × 3½"	White oak

This Arts and Crafts settee can be the centerpiece of any garden.

Greene & Greene Garden Bench

THIS UNDERSTATED GARDEN BENCH IS LIKE NO OTHER WE'VE SEEN. The fluid lines of the top and sides are inspired by the architectural work of the Greene brothers, who built houses and furniture around the turn of the century that are fast becoming national treasures. Yet this bench is surprisingly simple to build and will quickly catch the eye of everyone who visits your garden or solarium.

We used genuine mahogany for the bench, though you could easily substitute oak, teak or any other wood suitable for outdoors. (If you plan to use teak, be prepared to open that checkbook wide.) We bought our lumber already planed and surfaced for about $180. Purchasing rough stock would knock 30 percent to 40 percent off that price.

Start by laying out your crosscuts on the lumber. Because this bench has a lot of pieces, I marked each piece with a letter. Crosscut the lumber to rough length on a radial arm saw.

Take the wood to your jointer and edge joint one edge of each piece. This will give you a square, straightedge for ripping. Rip out the pieces at your table saw and then crosscut to the finished lengths in the Schedule of Materials.

Build the Back

Attaching the slats to the top cap and the bottom back rail requires a little math to get evenly spaced slats. You have 14 narrow slats that are 1½" wide, and three wider slats that are 2½" wide. The bottom back rail is 48" long. So subtract 21" from that 48" length to account for the small slats, and then subtract 7½" to account for the wide slats. This should leave you with 19½" for the spacing. Then divide this number by 16, which is the number of openings between the slats. This leaves 1 7/32" between each slat.

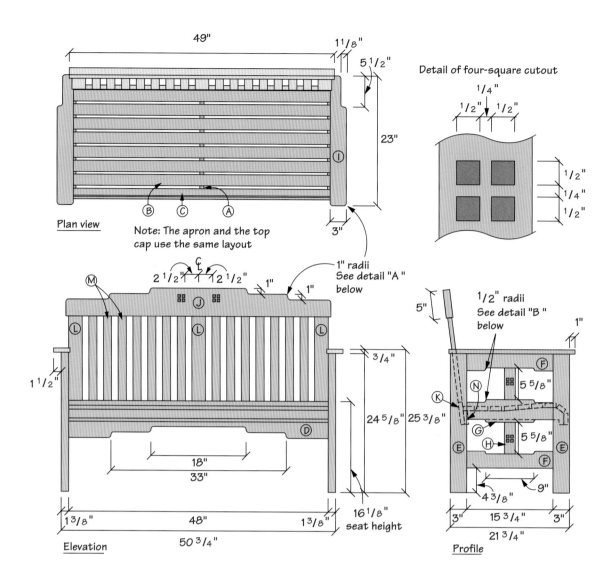

Plan view

Note: The apron and the top cap use the same layout

Detail of four-square cutout

Elevation

Profile

Details of cloud lift radii

Detail A

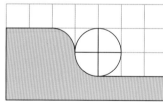

Detail B

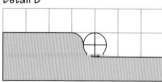

Each square = 1/2"

Enlarge 200%

Schedule of Materials: Greene & Greene Garden Bench

No.	Lett.	Item	Dimensions T W L	Material
3	A	Seat braces	$3/4" \times 3" \times 17^5/8"$	Mahogany
8	B	Seat slats	$3/4" \times 2" \times 48"$	Mahogany
1	C	Angled slat for seat	$3/4" \times 1^3/4" \times 48"$	Mahogany
1	D	Seat front apron	$3/4" \times 5" \times 48"$	Mahogany
4	E	Legs	$1^3/8" \times 3" \times 24^5/8"$	Mahogany
4	F	Upper & lower side rails	$3/4" \times 3" \times 15^3/4"$	Mahogany
2	G	Middle side rails	$3/4" \times 4" \times 15^3/4"$	Mahogany
4	H	Center side stiles	$3/4" \times 2" \times 5^5/8"$	Mahogany
2	I	Armrests	$3/4" \times 3" \times 23"$	Mahogany
1	J	Top cap	$1^1/4" \times 5" \times 49"$	Mahogany
2	K	Back bottom rail	$3/4" \times 4" \times 48"$	Mahogany
3	L	Wide back slats	$3/4" \times 2^1/2" \times 15"$	Mahogany
14	M	Narrow back slats	$3/4" \times 1^1/2" \times 15"$	Mahogany
1	N	Seat back rail	$3/4" \times 2^3/8" \times 48"$	Mahogany

Using a ruler with at least $^1/_{32}$" increments, lay out the locations for the dowel and biscuit cuts. Then, using a self-centering doweling jig, drill the $^1/_4$" dowel holes in the slats (two per slat end). Make sure the holes are just a shade deeper than the dowels you plan to use. This gives room for your glue to move.

Next, you need to lay out the slat locations on the top cap and bottom back rail. Here's how: Start at one end of the back rail and measure 2½" in from the end for the wider slats. Then measure out 1⅞₂" of space, then 1½" for the slat, then 1⅞₂" and so on until you've laid out seven narrow slats. Then start from the other side of the rail and lay out those seven narrow slats. The wider center slat is centered in what's left. The wider slats will be attached with biscuits; the narrow slats with dowels. To find the dowel centers on the back rail, measure in ¼" from the marks you made for the ends of each narrow slat. Drill the holes for the dowels on the bottom back rail as shown in the photo. Then lay out the holes on the top cap, keeping in mind it is 1" longer than the bottom back rail.

Cloud Lifts

Cut the cloud lift pattern on the top cap using the pattern in the diagram and a band saw. (Cloud lifts are soft, stair-stepped details.) Then cut the reverse cloud lift pattern on the apron that attaches to the front of the seat, as shown in the photo.

Straighten the Pattern

After you rough-cut the cloud lift shape on the band saw, straighten up the cuts on the table saw. When you're cleaning up the reverse cloud lift pattern, you need to be careful because you're going to have to raise and lower the table saw blade to get into the middle of the pattern. To finish the cloud lift pattern, use a ¼" roundover bit to cut a profile on the edges.

Assemble the Back

Now you have to do a little sanding. Using 120-grit sandpaper and a random orbit sander, sand the flat surfaces and break the edges of the back's slats. This will, in the end, give the piece a more finished look. It also has a practical purpose. If your bench is going to sit outside, the first spring shower or two will raise the grain of the wood. Squared edges will likely splinter, making your bench a potentially painful place to sit.

Attach the wider slats with biscuits; the narrower ones with dowels. Make your cuts for the biscuits on the wider slats and the back rails. After dry assembling the back, start with the bot-

First lay out the cloud lifts with a compass. Use a 1" Forstner bit to cut the inside radius on the top, apron and armrests. (Use a $^1/_2$" bit for the cloud lifts on the end pieces.)

tom rail. Paint your dowels with waterproof glue; insert them into the back rail. Then paint the other dowels' ends with glue and put a little glue on the end of the slat. Attach the slats. Then glue the dowels into the top back rail. Paint them with glue, put a little glue on the top end of each slat and attach the top rail. Clamp and let dry.

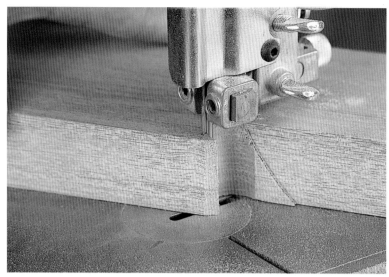

After you rough out the cloud lifts on a band saw, use a table saw to rip to the bottom of the inside radius cut on the drill press. (On the reverse cloud lifts for the apron, you need to set the ripping width with the table saw blade lowered below the table. With the saw running, hold the work firmly in place, making sure your hand is clear of the point where the blade will exit the piece. Then slowly raise the blade to make the interior cuts.) Then use your band saw to remove the waste on the outside radii. Clean up the cuts on a spindle sander.

Dry assemble the back to make sure everything lines up and that the back can be made square. Then, using clamping cauls, assemble the back with a waterproof glue (we used polyurethane glue). Check for square by measuring across the corners. The measurements should be identical. Then adjust the clamps accordingly.

Cut out the Square Patterns

The four-square pattern that goes on the back is repeated on the center stiles on the end. Mark the locations of the cutouts according to the diagram and lay out the location of the four squares.

Drill holes to make the pattern using a ½" Forstner bit. Clean up the holes with a jigsaw and a chisel.

Build the Ends

Begin building the ends by cutting the cloud lift and reverse cloud lift patterns on the top, bottom and middle rails with a band saw. Use the ¼" roundover bit on all the edges except those on the inside of the sides; these edges will be radiused after assembly.

After laying out the ends and cutting the cloud lifts on these parts, mark the pieces for the biscuit joiner cuts. Assemble the stiles and rails first. With this assembly clamped loosely, clamp the legs on; allow to dry. Polyurethane glue takes about four hours to dry and has a foamy squeeze-out.

Next make the cuts for your biscuits. These will attach the center stiles to the rails, and attach the rails to the legs. Make sure the rails and the legs are flush on the inside edge where they will attach to the seat. Use waterproof glue with the biscuits; clamp and set aside to dry.

Rout the Edges

When the glue is dry, use your router to radius the edges of the ends. Then cut out the armrests to the pattern shown in the diagram. Attach them to the end assemblies with screws, leaving a ⅛" overhang on the inside edge, and notch the arm to the back.

Seat Assembly

The first thing to do here is to cut out the three seat braces that support the seat's slats. Cutting the braces is a little tricky because several angles are at work here. We've included a pattern on page 81 to make things easier.

Once you've got the seat braces cut, make the seat's back rail. This piece runs along the entire back of the bench

Lay out and drill the four-square cutouts using a ¹/₂" Forstner bit in a drill press. Square the corners using a jigsaw. Square the openings with a sharp chisel.

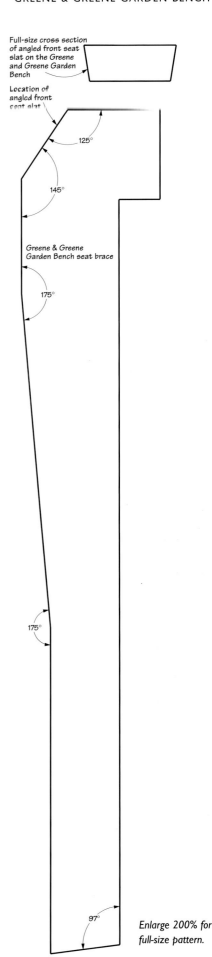

Full-size cross section of angled front seat slat on the Greene and Greene Garden Bench

Location of angled front seat slat

125°

145°

Greene & Greene Garden Bench seat brace

175°

175°

97°

Enlarge 200% for full-size pattern.

After the ends are dry, use a ¼" roundover bit to radius all of the edges — except the top where the armrest will be attached. Using a four-in-hand rasp and starting at a 45-degree angle to the corner, gently file out a mitered corner. Remove burn marks from the corners with the rasp and finish the corners with sandpaper.

After the slats are screwed in, flip the seat over and lay the front apron against the front slat. Mark the locations of the seat braces onto the apron. Using a backsaw and chisel, cut 2" x ¾" notches into the apron. Attach the apron to the back of the front slat with screws and glue. You also need to cut a ⅞" x 16" cutaway into the ends of the seat braces. This starts at the back of the seat brace and keeps the seat brace from peeking below the cloud lift on the ends.

and is the place where the bench's back and the seat are joined. To make the back tip at a comfortable angle, cut a bevel on both edges of this piece. Set the angle of your table saw's blade to 7 degrees. Run one edge through. Then flip the piece over lengthwise and run the other edge through, creating a parallel cut to the first one.

While you're at the table saw, set the blade's angle to 10 degrees. Take the 1½"-wide seat slat and run one edge

through the saw to create a bevel. Then flip the piece onto its other face and run the other edge through. The result is one face that is narrower than the other. This seat slat goes on the highest part of the seat, and the bevel will make the seat more comfortable.

Then, using screws and waterproof glue, attach the three seat braces to the seat's back rail. Then take one of the 2" slats for the seat and attach it to the front of the three seat braces with

screws and waterproof glue. Screw and glue the rest of the slats as shown in the photo, making sure to attach the beveled 1½" slat to the highest point of the seat.

The diagram on page 81 shows the shape of the seat braces. Attach the tapered seat slat to the front angle on the seat brace. Then, using galvanized screws, attach the remaining seat slats, leaving about 7⁄16" between each slat.

Notch the Apron

When I designed the front apron, I intended it to be merely decorative. However, after some experimentation, I decided it could help hold up the seat. To attach it to the seat, cut three 2" × ¾" notches into the front rail, and screw the front rail into the seat behind the front rail. Use a sharp chisel to cut a screw pocket on the back face of the apron near each end. This is where you will attach the apron to the legs.

Assembly

Screw the back bottom rail to the seat's back rail with eight screws. Place one of the bench's end assemblies flat on the floor. Using a square, measure where the seat brace attaches to the seat's side rail and mark a line. Then mark three biscuit cuts that will attach the back leg to the end of the back. Mark both sides of the back on the leg.

Attach the Ends

Attach the seat assembly to the back leg with biscuits. Then, from the inside of the bench, screw the seat brace to the seat's side rail using 1¼" screws. Be careful not to countersink too much, or the screw will go through both thicknesses of wood.

Then use a 1⅝" galvanized screw to screw the apron to the leg in the screw pocket you cut earlier. Repeat this procedure for the other side assembly. You can finish this bench with varnish or an outdoor-safe polyurethane. I chose to leave the wood bare so it will slowly turn a silvery gray.

This bench looks great in the garden or solarium and will last for years outdoors, but some of you might opt to keep yours in the front hall or near the back door.

Clamp the seat assembly to the back, making sure the back is flush to the bottom of the seat. Screw the two together with 1¼" galvanized screws and glue. Then, on the inside of the ends, lay out the location of the seat braces. The seat brace starts 13" up from the bottom of the leg to the inside of the cutaway.

Clamp a straight piece of wood to the front line on the leg. Then using a biscuit jointer with the fence removed, make your biscuit cuts.

This classy companion piece to the garden bench in the preceding
chapter looks great on the patio or in your living room.

Greene & Greene Patio Table

A READER FROM CLAREMONT, CALIFORNIA, EVERETT VINZANT, liked *Popular Wood-working* magazine's Greene & Greene garden bench in the May 1997 issue of *Popular Woodworking* so much he de-cided to build a coffee table to go with it. He sent us a photo of it, and we de-cided it was such a good idea we tweaked his nice design and built this table. We call this project "Revenge of the Cloud Lifts" because it's loaded with this undulating signature Arts and Crafts detail. Because there are so many cloud lifts, this is a good project to use template routing on a router table to make them all.

Making Templates
Begin by cutting the parts out according to the Schedule of Materials. Then make your plywood templates using the pat-terns on page 87. Mark a center line across each template; this will help you line up the parts for routing. Finish each template by adding two handles to the templates in the locations shown on page 87.

Roughing the Parts
Mark a center line across parts B, C, D, F, G, K and on two top slats (J). Mark a center line down the middle and across parts E and K. These get a four-hole cutout. Make four copies of the small four-hole cutout and one of the larger four-hole patterns shown on page 87. Cut the patterns to within ½" of the holes. Using a spray adhesive, attach the small patterns on the end uprights (E) and the large pattern on the center slat (K), lining up the crosshairs on the pat-tern with the crosshairs on the parts. Drill ¼" clearance holes in each hole and cut out the squares with a scroll saw. You can't quite cut all of the holes on the center slat but come close and clean up the rest with a chisel.

Routing the Parts
Mount a ⅜" pattern bit into a router table and set the depth of the bearing to run against the template while cut-ting the part.

Biscuits and Assembly
After routing the cloud lifts, cut all of the biscuit joints for the base and top. I used Porter-Cable's new biscuit joiner for this table because it comes with a 2" blade perfect for joining the base and top parts with smaller biscuits.

The easiest way to lay out the biscuit joints is to dry clamp the end assembly together and mark the centers of the ends on the apron pieces and legs. The aprons have a ¼" setback from the out-side of the legs, so cut the biscuit slots on the apron assembly first. Then, using a ¼" spacer, set up the biscuit joiner to cut the offset on the legs. Use no. 20 biscuits on the short aprons (C) and Porter-Cable face frame biscuits (or dowels) on the end dividers and up-rights (D and E). Before assembly, rout a ¼" radius on the legs and the ends of the apron parts that contact the legs.

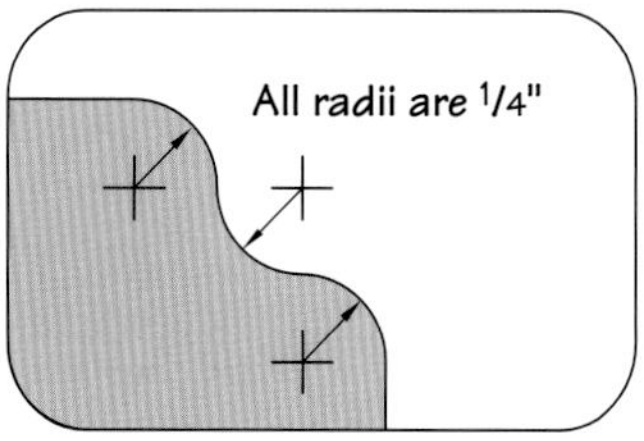
All radii are 1/4"

Full-size detail of corner profile

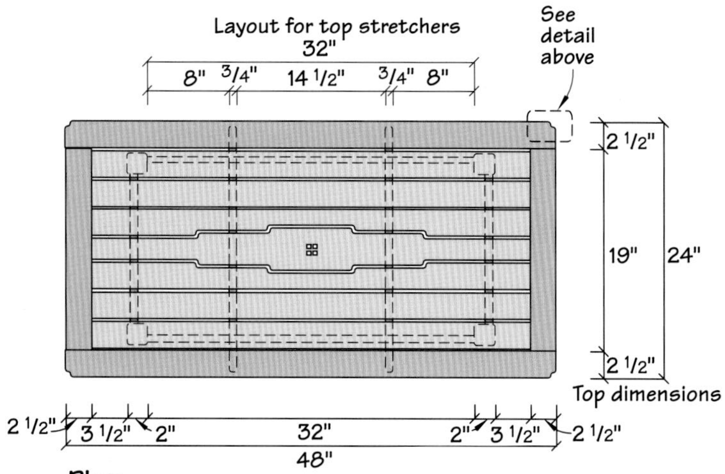
Layout for top stretchers
32"
8" 3/4" 14 1/2" 3/4" 8"
See detail above
2 1/2"
19"
24"
2 1/2"
Top dimensions
2 1/2" 3 1/2" 2" 32" 2" 3 1/2" 2 1/2"
48"

Plan

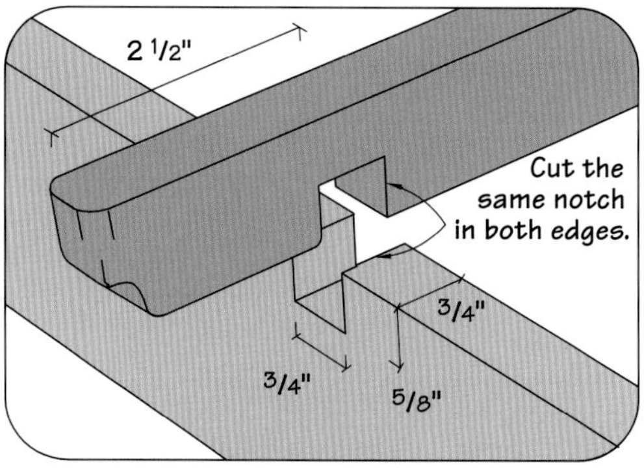
2 1/2"
Cut the same notch in both edges.
3/4"
3/4"
5/8"

Detail of top stretcher

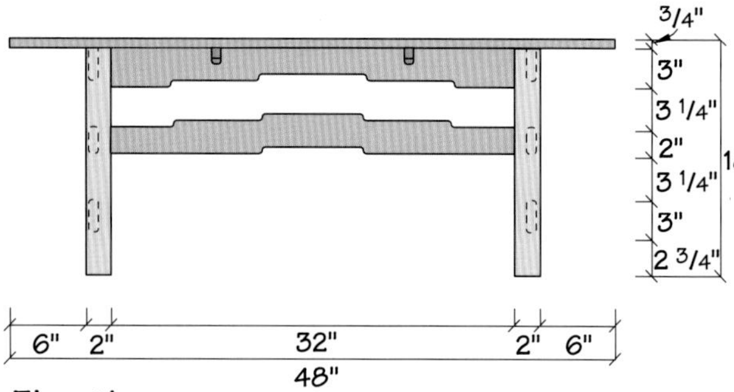
3/4"
3"
3 1/4"
2"
3 1/4"
3"
2 3/4"
18"
6" 2" 32" 2" 6"
48"

Elevation

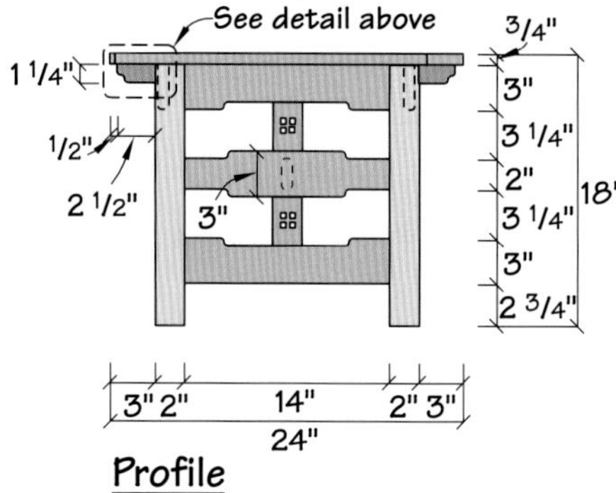
See detail above
1 1/4"
1/2"
2 1/2"
3"
3/4"
3"
3 1/4"
2"
3 1/4"
3"
2 3/4"
18"
3" 2" 14" 2" 3"
24"

Profile

Rout the rest of the assembly after gluing up. One last step before assembly is to drill screw pockets into the upper aprons for attaching the top. Glue up the end assembly.

After drying, mark the location of the base stretcher on each end assembly. Take the long aprons and base stretcher and dry clamp the entire base together. The base stretcher should be press fit between the end assemblies. Repeat the same process of cutting #20 biscuit slots on the long aprons and end assemblies. Dowel the base stretcher into each end assembly using two ⅜" dowels. After doweling the stretcher,

Schedule of Materials: Greene & Greene Patio Table

No.	Lett.	Item	Dimensions T W L	Material
4	A	Legs	2" x 2" x 17¼"	Mahogany
2	B	Long aprons	¾" x 3" x 32"	Mahogany
4	C	Short aprons	¾" x 3" x 14"	Mahogany
2	D	End divider	¾" x 3" x 14"	Mahogany
4	E	End uprights	¾" x 2" x 3¼"	Mahogany
1	F	Base stretcher	¾" x 3" x 34"	Mahogany
2	G	Top stretchers	¾" x 1¼" 23"	Mahogany
2	H	Top frame long	¾" x 2½" x 48"	Mahogany
2	I	Top frame short	¾" x 2½" x 19"	Mahogany
6	J	Top slats	¾" x 2½" x 43"	Mahogany
1	K	Center slat	¾" x 3" x 43"	Mahogany

Full-size diagram of both four-hole cutouts,
the double radius on the top stretcher and top, the layout
for all of the cloud lifts on the table and a scale
diagram of the jig used for routing the cloud lifts.

Top stretcher

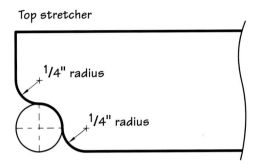

1/4" radius

1/4" radius

Full-size diagram of double radius
on the top stretcher and top

Top cutouts

End assembly cutouts

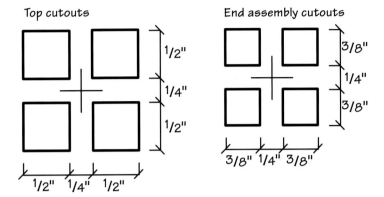

1/2"

1/4"

1/2"

3/8"

1/4"

3/8"

3/8" 1/4" 3/8"

1/2" 1/4" 1/2"

Full-size diagram of four hole cutouts in the top and end assemblies

Full-size diagram of the cloud lifts. Use this to lay out the
individual cloud lifts on the jig above. Each square equals 1".

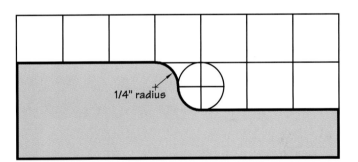

1/4" radius

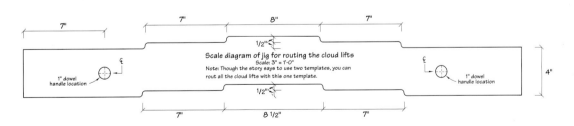

7" 7" 8" 7"

1/2"

Scale diagram of jig for routing the cloud lifts
Scale: 3" = 1'-0"
Note: Though the story says to use two templates, you can
rout all the cloud lifts with this one template.

1/2"

1" dowel handle location

1" dowel handle location

4"

7" 8 1/2" 7"

Enlarge 200% for full-size pattern.

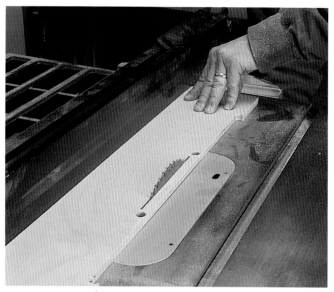

Begin cutting out the ¹/₂" Baltic birch templates by drilling holes at the proper corners. Raise the blade on the table saw into the middle of the stock to make the straight cuts. Band saw the rest and clean up the cloud lifts using a disc sander.

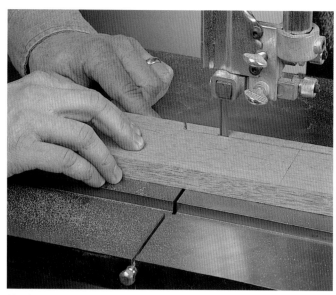

Use the center lines to index the template on what will be the back of each piece (it will eventually have nails driven into it) and draw the appropriate cloud lift or reverse cloud lift. Cutting close to the line, rough out these pieces on the band saw.

Pattern-routing the parts is easy using the templates. Nail the appropriate template to a roughed-out part, using the index lines for reference. Begin routing with the bit cutting against the wood. When you come to a cloud lift, use a climb cut so you don't burn the rounded corner.

Lay out a ⁵/₈"-deep by ³/₄"-wide notch into the top stretcher and the base. The notch is 2³/₄" in from the stretcher end and 8" in from the joint where the apron meets the leg. Notice the clearance holes drilled into the top edge of the base and stretcher.

lay out and scroll saw the profile on the ends of the top stretchers using the pattern on page 87. Let the top stretchers into the base using half-lap joints according to the diagram. Then glue the entire base together and screw the stretchers into the top edge of the base.

Begin the top assembly by routing a ¼" radius on the top long edge of all the slats. Using ¼" spacers, clamp the slats together without glue. Dry clamp the

ends in place and mark for biscuit joints. Cut the biscuit slots and glue this top subassembly together. When it's dry, place the long top frame pieces against the subassembly and mark the inside corner where the short frame meets the long frame. Rout a ¼" radius on the inside edge of the long frame piece between the corner marks. With a rasp, finish the radius where it tapers on the ends. Mark and cut biscuit slots,

then glue up the top. After drying, cut a profile on each corner using the pattern for the top stretchers. Rout a ¼" radius on the outside edge of the top.

After sanding, center the base on the underside of the top and attach it to the top using 1½" screws in the screw pockets and 1¾" screws in the top stretchers. No finish is required. If you leave the table unfinished and outdoors, it will turn a beautiful silver color.

This charming piece features a Mackintosh influence emphasized by its flower motif.

Bungalow Mailbox

THIS PROJECT WAS BY REQUEST. As I live in the 'burbs and have to walk to the curb to pick up my bills, a mailbox mounted next to my front door would be purely decorative. But a friend lucky enough to have postal delivery right to his door asked if I could come up with an appropriate design for his Arts and Crafts–style bungalow home.

After a little research I settled on a design reminiscent of the work of Charles Rennie Mackintosh. Arguably Scotland's greatest 20th-century architect and designer, Mackintosh inspired much of the European Arts and Crafts movement during the early 1900s. A stylized flower motif is found on many of his pieces.

Mostly Glue

The joinery for the box is primarily glue and butt joints, utilizing the long-grain-to-long-grain orientation of the sides,

The bottom fits into the front and back pieces using a tongue-and-groove method. The sides are not attached to the bottom, and in fact the bottom is cut to allow a $^1/_{16}$" gap on either side. Should water happen to get into the mailbox, these gaps will allow it to escape rather than pool up in the bottom.

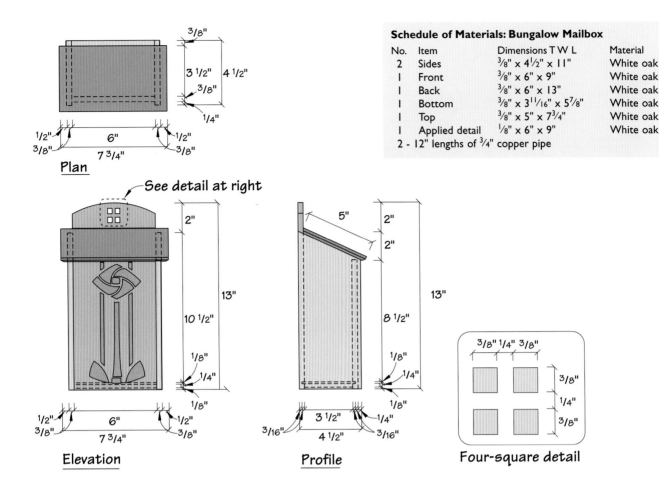

No.	Item	Dimensions T W L	Material
2	Sides	$3/8$" x $4^1/2$" x 11"	White oak
1	Front	$3/8$" x 6" x 9"	White oak
1	Back	$3/8$" x 6" x 13"	White oak
1	Bottom	$3/8$" x $3^{11}/16$" x $5^7/8$"	White oak
1	Top	$3/8$" x 5" x $7^3/4$"	White oak
1	Applied detail	$1/8$" x 6" x 9"	White oak

Schedule of Materials: Bungalow Mailbox

2 - 12" lengths of $3/4$" copper pipe

Plan

Elevation

Profile

Four-square detail

back and front. The bottom, however, sits in a tongue-and-groove joint between the front and back pieces to allow the wood to move.

After cutting the pieces according to the Schedule of Materials, cut a $1/4$" × $1/8$" rabbet on the underside of the two long edges of the bottom. This will leave a $1/8$" × $1/8$" tongue on the front and back of the bottom (page 89, left). Then cut the dadoes on the inside bottom of the front and back pieces by setting the rip fence for $1/2$" and the blade height to $3/16$" (page 89, right).

Adding the Angles
Now cut the sides of the mailbox on an angle so you can attach the mailbox to your house without cramming a tool inside the box. The sides slope at a 25-degree angle with the front edge measuring 9" tall and the back edge 11" tall.

Now cut the chamfer on the underside of the lid. The front and two sides are chamfered at a 45-degree angle on

the table saw, leaving a $3/16$" flat edge to the top of the lid. The back edge of the lid is cut at a 25-degree angle to mate with the box's back.

Detailing the Back
To add another Mackintosh feature, I cut a four-square pattern centered in the top of the curved back.

First mark the location of the four-square pattern as shown on the diagram. Use a $3/8$" drill bit to remove most of the waste from the squares. Then use a chisel and a triangular file to clean up the cuts. To make the curve, draw a 6" radius along the top edge of the back and cut to the mark on the band saw.

After sanding, you're ready to glue up the box. The front is set back $1/4$" on the sides, while the back is flush to the back edge. The bottom is left loose in the assembly.

Now cut out the applied detail from $1/8$" stock on the scroll saw. A full-size pattern is provided on page 91.

Finishing Touches
Before gluing the flower to the box, stain the box a rustic-looking gray-brown by applying a black aniline dye wash. The wash was made by diluting the dye eight-to-one with denatured alcohol. I then colored the flower and stem pieces with undiluted aniline dye. Attach the flower pieces using cyanoacrylate glue. To finish, use a coat of spar urethane for outdoor protection.

The final tasks are installing a small jewelry box continuous hinge for the lid and the copper magazine hooks. I made the hooks from a couple pieces of $3/4$" copper tubing. Flatten the piece with a dead-blow hammer, then use a ball-peen hammer to add a dimpled, hand-hammered appearance. I then antiqued the copper using a product called Patina Green from a company called Modern Options, (415) 252-5580. The product quickly adds a nice green patina.

Now screw the two hooks to the back, and the mailbox is ready to hang.

The top is chamfer cut on three edges, and angle cut on the back edge.

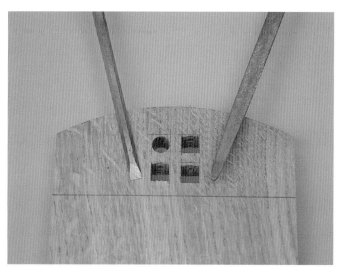

After drilling the holes, use a ¼"chisel and a triangular file to clean up the hole. The top left hole is shown after drilling, while the other three holes have been completed.

Full-size diagram of rose and stem/leaf parts

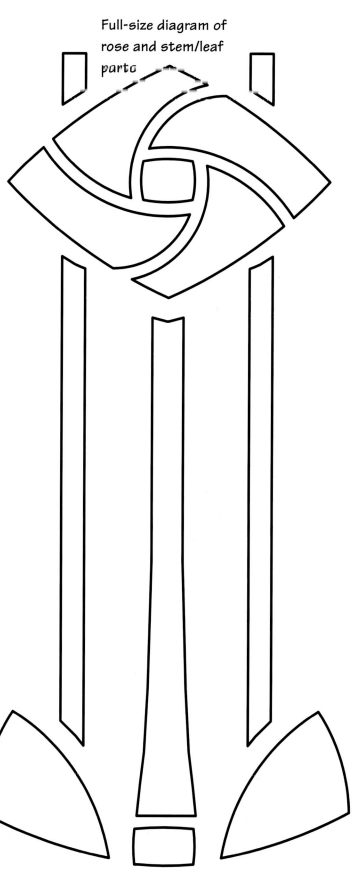

By combining some classic **Arts and Crafts** elements,
and store-bought works, a new classic is born.

Mantel Clock

You might not be ready to build your own sideboard, but you can start your Arts and Crafts collection with this simple clock. The only tough part of the project is finding a great piece of quarter-sawn white oak (1" × 6" × 96").

First Things First

Cut the pieces according to the Schedule of Materials. Resaw and book match the front for an impressive appearance. Taper the front to an 8" width at the top. Then, crosscut a 4-degree angle on the top and bottom edges of both sides, parallel to one another.

Cut the Front

Cut the dial hole and pendulum slots in the front (see page 93 for pattern). Use a chamfer bit to cut the angle profile in the dial hole.

Cut the Top and Bottom

To cut the top and bottom chamfer details (including the ⅛" bead), use your table saw. Start by making a ⅛"-deep cut 1" in on the ends and front edges. Cut the bevel by running the pieces on edge (use a zero-clearance throat plate) with the blade set to 23 degrees. Set the blade height to intersect with the bead cut and set the fence to leave the ³⁄₁₆" flat shown in the diagram. To inset the front ¼" back from the sides, lay it on a ¼" piece of Masonite as a spacer; glue the two sides to the face. The fall-off pieces from the front taper make perfect clamping cauls to exert equal pres-

Schedule of Materials: Mantel Clock

No.	Item	Dimensions T W L	Material
1	Front	$\frac{1}{2}$" x 9" x 14"	White oak
1	Bottom	$\frac{3}{4}$" x 5" x 12"	White oak
1	Top	$\frac{3}{4}$" x 5" x 10"	White oak
2	Sides	$\frac{1}{2}$" x $3^{15}/_{16}$" x $14\frac{1}{8}$"	White oak
1	Back	$\frac{1}{4}$" x $9\frac{7}{8}$" x $14^{9}/_{16}$"	Oak plywood
1	Dial support	$\frac{3}{4}$" x $5\frac{1}{2}$" x 6"	Pine
4	Fake tenons	$\frac{1}{4}$" x $\frac{1}{2}$" x $1\frac{1}{2}$"	White oak
8	Fake pins	$\frac{1}{8}$" x $\frac{1}{4}$" x $\frac{1}{4}$"	White oak

SUPPLIES

1 - Dial face
Woodcraft
(800) 225-1153 or www.woodcraft.com
Item # 124985 • $1.99 each
1 - Mechanism
Item # 124898 • $9.99 each

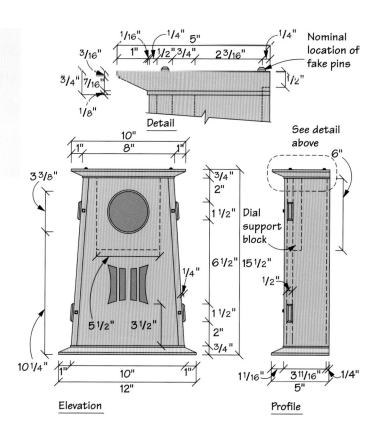

Detail

Elevation

Profile

sure on the sides. Pilot-drill, then nail the bottom and top to the sides, leaving a $\frac{1}{16}$" setback. Set the nails.

Through-tenons

Cut, chamfer, then glue the applied through-tenons as located on the diagrams. Cut, chamfer and glue the fake square pegs to cover the nail holes. Rout a $\frac{1}{4}$" by $\frac{3}{8}$"-deep rabbet in the clock's back edges. Then fit the back into the rabbet.

The Block and Face

Cut the dial support block and glue the clock face to the block, centered and $2\frac{1}{2}$" down from the top of the block. Apply two coats of clear finish to the block and face, which is typically paper.

Attach the Hands

Drill a hole in the center of the clock face for attaching the hands to the clock mechanism and attach the movement to the back of the support block.

Apply Glaze and Finish

To finish, first apply warm brown glaze to the clock case. Apply a few coats of clear finish.

Last Things Last

Screw the dial support block to the inside of the face. Shorten and attach the pendulum, then pilot-drill the back and attach using no. 4 × $\frac{3}{4}$" brass screws.

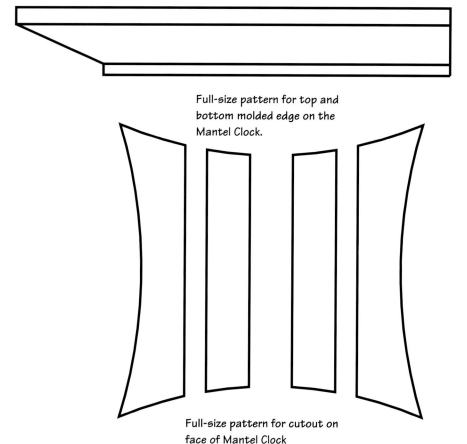

Full-size pattern for top and bottom molded edge on the Mantel Clock.

Full-size pattern for cutout on face of Mantel Clock

This extremely rare wall cabinet is an excellent project for beginning woodworkers.

Byrdcliffe Wall Cabinet

THE FURNITURE BUILT BY THE BYRD-CLIFFE ARTS COLONY between 1903 and 1905 is rare, unusual and expensive. Luckily, it's cheap and easy to build at home.

Instead of pricey quartersawn white oak, many Byrdcliffe pieces were built from inexpensive poplar. And instead of the fussy ammonia-fuming process used by many Arts and Crafts manufacturers to color their furniture, many Byrdcliffe pieces were left uncolored to show off the grain. Our project is inspired by a hanging cabinet that sold at auction for $3,740.

Build the Case

Cut the pieces to size according to the Schedule of Materials. Cut a ¼" × ¾" rabbet in the back of the cabinet using your table saw. Presand the cabinet parts, then assemble the frame with biscuits or dowels. Make sure the shelf and divider are flush to the front of the cabinet. Glue and clamp until dry.

Stub Tenon Door

Next rip the rails and stiles for the door, making a ¼"-wide by ⅝"-deep groove in the center of one long edge of all four pieces to receive the panel. The groove also holds the tenons in the rails. Then cut ¼" × ⁹⁄₁₆" tenons on both ends of the door's rails using a dado stack. Cut a ¼" × ½" rabbet on all four edges of the panel. Sand the parts, then assemble the door with the rabbet facing the back of the door. Glue and clamp.

Solid Back

Glue up the poplar for the back. When it's dry, nail the back into place. Be sure

Schedule of Materials: Byrdcliffe Wall Cabinet

No.	Item	Dimensions T W L	Material
2	Sides	¾" × 8" × 18"	Poplar
2	Top & bottom	¾" × 8" × 37½"	Poplar
1	Shelf	¾" × 7¼" × 27¼"	Poplar
1	Divider	¾" × 7¼" × 16½"	Poplar
1	Back	¾" × 17⅛" × 38⅛"	Poplar
2	Rails	¾" × 2¼" × 6"	Poplar
2	Stiles	¾" × 2¼" × 16½"	Poplar
1	Panel	½" × 6" × 13"	Poplar

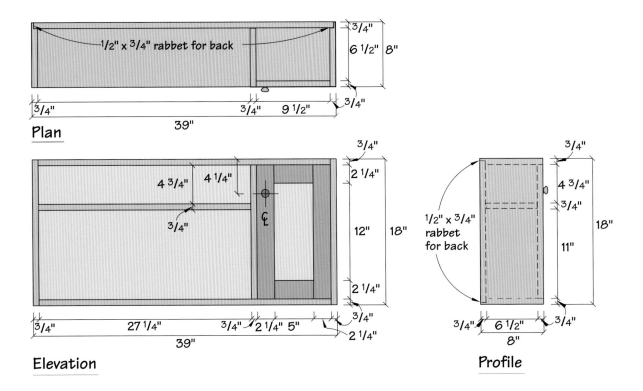

Plan

1/2" x 3/4" rabbet for back

3/4"
6 1/2" 8"
3/4"
3/4" 9 1/2"
39"

Elevation

4 3/4" 4 1/4"
3/4"
27 1/4" 3/4" 2 1/4" 5"
2 1/4"
39"

3/4"
2 1/4"
12" 18"
2 1/4"
3/4"

Profile

1/2" x 3/4" rabbet for back

3/4"
4 3/4"
3/4"
11" 18"
3/4" 6 1/2" 3/4"
8"

to allow some space for the back to expand. If you want to make the cabinet weigh less, use ½" poplar plywood for the back, but be sure to then cut the shelf and divider ¼" wider. Don't use less than ½" plywood if you plan to hang the cabinet by screwing through the back.

Finishing Touches

Cut mortises for the hinges and hang the door before finishing. Finish sand the cabinet. The best way to stain the cabinet green is by spraying on aniline dye diluted with alcohol. I used an inexpensive Preval Power Unit aerosol can (about $4 at craft and hardware stores). After you spray the dye on, wipe it down immediately with a rag moistened with denatured alcohol to minimize blotching.

Scroll Saw Flower

Cut the iris flower pattern from ¼" poplar with a scroll saw or coping saw (see pattern). Dye the pieces, then glue them to the panel with a superglue. Cover the cabinet with two coats of clear finish.

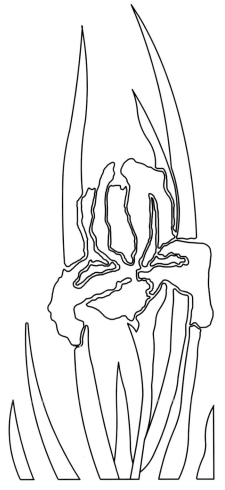

Enlarge 200% for full-size pattern.

Heirloom Cradle

BELIEVE IT OR NOT, the wood in this cradle was cut from a fruit bearing cherry tree from my parent's back-yard in Bloomsburg, Pennsylvania. I don't remember the tree, but there are photos of my father and me (still in diapers) in front of it. Dad had to cut the tree down a short time after the photos were taken, but he hauled it to a sawmill, and stored the rough-cut lumber in our garage.

Twenty-five years later, my wife and I were expecting our first baby, so Dad and I figured out a cradle design and pulled out some of that wood that was still in the garage. The old photos, the old wood, a new baby and a new design have created an heirloom.

Laminate the Legs
The lumber I had on hand forced me to laminate the legs and feet to yield the necessary 1½" × 3" pieces, but you may have thicker stock available. I planed the other pieces to ¾" or ⅝" thick, then cut them to width and length according to the Schedule of Materials. When laminating the legs and feet, allow extra material for additional milling in steps eight and nine.

End Frames
To form the end frames, cut a 6-degree angle on the ends of the stiles and rails so that the end frames are slightly trapezoidal. The center slats each have one long edge tapered on a 6-degree angle so that its edges are all parallel to the frame pieces.

Join End Frames
Join the end frames with half-lap joints where the stiles and rails meet. The two center slats and the center stile overlap and are recessed into the rails from the inside (see diagram). I used a ⅛"

straight bit in a router to recess the slats into the rails.

Sand For a Round Effect
I was inspired by Greene & Greene fur-niture, and by rounding the corners with a disc sander, I attained a similar look. All the edges are then rounded with a quarter-round router bit. To hang

97

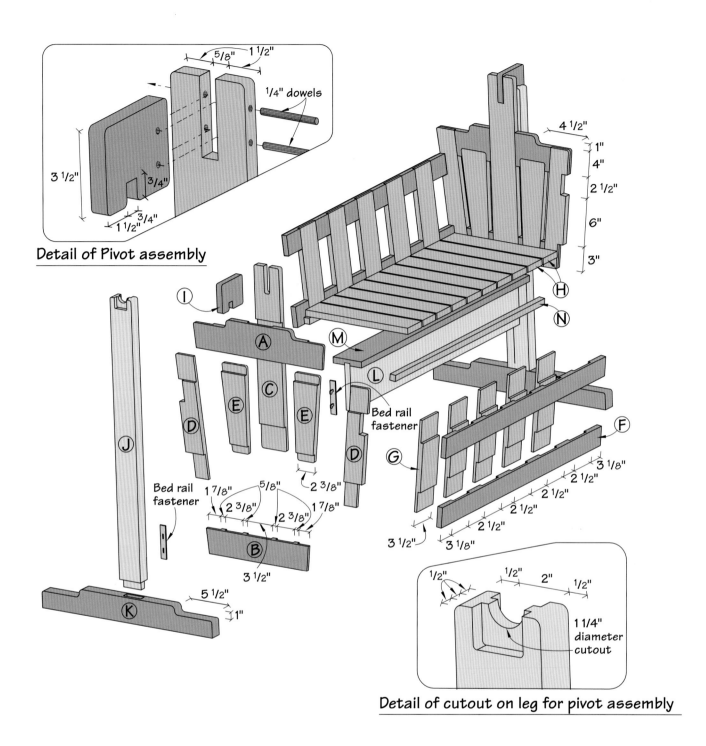

Detail of Pivot assembly

5/8" 1 1/2"

1/4" dowels

3 1/2"

3/4"

1 1/2" 3/4"

4 1/2"

1"

4"

2 1/2"

6"

3"

H

N

I

A

M

E

C

E

D

D

L

Bed rail
fastener

J

G

F

Bed rail
fastener

1 7/8" 5/8"

2 3/8"

2 3/8" 1 7/8"

B

3 1/2"

3 1/8"

2 1/2"

2 1/2"

2 1/2"

2 1/2"

3 1/8"

3 1/2"

3 1/8"

2 3/8"

5 1/2"

1"

K

1/2" 1/2" 2" 1/2"

1 1/4"
diameter
cutout

Detail of cutout on leg for pivot assembly

Schedule of Materials: Heirloom Cradle

No.	Lett.	Item	Dimensions T W L	Material
2	A	End rails (top)	$5/8$" × 4" × $18^{1}/2$"	Cherry
1	B	End rails (bottom)	$5/8$" × 3" × 16"	Cherry
2	C	Center stiles	$5/8$" × $3^{1}/2$" × 22"	Cherry
4	D	End stiles	$5/8$" × $2^{1}/2$" × $14^{5}/8$"	Cherry
4	E	Center slats	$5/8$" × $3^{1}/2$" × $10^{1}/2$"	Cherry
4	F	Side rails	$5/8$" × $2^{1}/2$" × 34"	Cherry
10	G	Side slats	$5/8$" × $3^{1}/2$" × 11"	Cherry
10	H	Bottom slats	$5/8$" × 3" × $14^{3}/8$"	Cherry
2	I	Pivot pieces	$5/8$" × $3^{1}/2$" × $4^{1}/2$"	Cherry
2	J	Legs	$1^{1}/2$" × 3" × $33^{3}/4$"	Cherry
2	K	Feet	$1^{1}/2$" × 3" × 24"	Cherry
1	L	Stretcher rail	$3/4$" × $5^{3}/8$" × 36"	Cherry
1	M	Stretcher cap	$3/4$" × 4" × 36"	Cherry
2	N	Cleats	$3/4$" × $3/4$" × 32"	Cherry

SUPPLIES

4" Heavy-duty bed
rail fasteners
Woodworkers Supply
(800) 645-9292
Item # 125-061 • $8.75
for a package of 4 sets

Rockler Woodworking
(800) 279-4441 or
www.rockler.com
General Finishes'
Toymaker's Finish

the basket, cut a $5/8$" × $3^{1}/2$" notch centered in the top end of the center stiles to hold the pivot pieces. I used a doweling jig to drill holes through the width of the center stiles to accept a $1/4$" maple dowel. Dowel the pieces together and trim the ends flush.

Prepare the Frames

Dry assemble the end frames, and mark and notch the frames to accept the side rails as shown in the diagram. Cut half-laps on the ends of each side slat, then notch the rails to match.

Attach Side and End Frames

Sand all pieces to 220-grit and glue up the end and side frames. Attach the side frames to the end frames using countersunk $1^{1}/4$" no. 6 wood screws, filling the holes with walnut dowel plugs for contrast. Cut the two support cleats and screw them to the inside, about $1/2$" up from the bottom of the basket. Next, countersink holes in the bottom slats, and glue and screw the bottom slats to the cleats.

Mortise and Tenon

Attach the legs to the feet with a mortise-and-tenon joint. Cut a 1"-deep by 1" by $2^{1}/2$" mortise in the center of each foot. Then cut the tenons on the legs to fit.

Pivot Piece

To form the notch in the legs that the pivot piece rests in, drill a $1^{1}/4$" diameter hole centered 1" down from the top. Then cut 1" off that end, giving you a $5/8$" notch in the end to support the basket.

The pivot piece and leg fit together in a loose bridle joint. You will need to cut a $3/4$" × $3/4$" notch in the pivot piece, then cut a $1/2$" deep recess around the notch on the inside and outside faces of the legs (see diagram detail).

Make Mortises

To allow for easier transport, attach the legs and stretcher with knockdown bed hardware. Mark and mortise the legs and stretcher ends for the hardware. I used a router with a $1/8$" spiral bit to make these mortises.

Attach the Stretcher Cap

To attach the stretcher cap, cut a $3/4$"-wide by $1/4$"-deep groove down the center of the stretcher cap. I used a dado head on the table saw to make the groove, then glued and clamped the cap in place.

Finishing Up

To finish the piece in a baby-friendly manner, sand all the pieces to 220-grit, then apply three coats of General Finishes' Toymaker's Finish, a wipe-on oil finish, buffing lightly with 400-grit sandpaper between coats.

This essential piece of dining room furniture is slightly scaled down to fit today's household demands and dimensions.

Sideboard

Photo by Al Parrish • Thanks to the Heidenreich family of Cincinnati, Ohio.

WHEN THE ARTS & CRAFTS MOVEMENT SWEPT AMERICA IN THE EARLY 1900s, furniture scale was anything but diminutive. Houses had 10'-high ceilings, and even the "modest" bungalow of the time had larger spaces for living (but much smaller spaces for sleeping) than today's typical tract house. Common sizes for sideboards at that time were 38" to the top, 24" deep and anywhere from 40" to 80" in length. In today's 12' × 12' dining area, that's just too large. I scaled mine down to 34" to the top, 19" in depth and 66" in length. Some of the construction has been updated, as well, using biscuits where appropriate and plywood panels.

As with most Arts and Crafts pieces, wood selection and hardware are the features that bring the simple construction to life. The material for the legs, top, sides, drawer faces and doors should be carefully selected from quarter-sawn white oak to provide the largest, most uniform ray flake possible.

Start Construction With the Side Panels

After choosing your lumber for the most dramatic effect, begin construction by cutting the legs to size and marking the locations of the ½" by 2" by ¾"-deep mortises for the three 3"-wide rails. In addition, the back legs get a ¼" × ¼" groove on the inside face for the backs to slip into. The side panels are assembled using tongue-and-groove construction. Set your table saw to run a ½"-deep center groove down the inside edge of the stiles and rails. Make the groove wide enough to allow your ¼" panels to fit snugly without forcing. Then reset your saw to cut ¼" × ½" tongues on both ends of the top side rails, and the bottom of each stile.

The final step on the lower rails is to draw an arch 1" up from the bottom of the rail, running from side to side. Cut the arches on both lower rails using a jigsaw, then sand the edges smooth. Next, cut the panels to size (leave ¹⁄₁₆" clearance all the way around the panels so they won't interfere with assembly). Prior to assembling the sides, finish sand both sides of the panels and the inside edge of the stiles and rails. Then glue up the parts, putting only a spot of glue on the panels.

Attaching the Rails

The next step is to cut and prepare the rails that will divide the drawers and run between the two side panels. The long rails (one oak and two poplar) are the same size and can be cut and tenoned at the same time. Once the tenons are complete, the front rail gets a 1" arch as on the sides. The two back rails each get a ½" × ½" rabbet to hold the back pieces and partitions.

I made the rest of the rails and the two center partitions out of plywood with a 1" solid oak front edge. With the rails and partitions edged, cut notches in the front edge of the two partitions and the back edge of the long drawer

For the half-blind dovetails, I used the $20 jig method outlined in Troy Sexton's article in the September 1999 issue of Popular Woodworking. It seemed like a clever idea when we ran the article, so I had to try it for myself. The scrap-wood templates and router template guide worked great. There's a different template for each row of drawers, but the templates are quick and easy to make.

The sides are where everything comes together with the three mortises, the back slot and finally the biscuit joint for the long drawer rail.

rail to form a bridle joint. This provides strength and rigidity to the rails and allows the grain of the top rail to run the width of the cabinet without interruption. Also, the top back corner of each partition requires a ½" × 3" notch for the top rear rail to attach.

Join the three drawer rails to the cabinet with biscuits — the two short rails between the two partitions, and the long one between the two side panels. When cutting the biscuits in the side panels, remember that the drawers, partitions and drawer rails are set back ⅜" from the legs.

Next mark the bottom piece and the front and back lower rails for biscuits, attaching the rails flush to the top surface of the bottom piece. Then glue the rails in place to the bottom. Pay careful attention to the length of the bottom at the rail tenons.

Now clamp the center drawer section together and mark the partition locations on the bottom piece. Then drill clearance holes through the bottom for the screws to attach the partitions to the bottom.

The next step requires a little juggling and an extra pair of hands. Glue the rails between the two partitions, then screw the partitions to the bottom. Now put the front rail in place in the partition's bridle joint, and glue and tap the bottom tenons in place in the side panel mortises. Leave the top splayed open to glue the biscuits and tenons for the rear top rail and the long drawer rail. Tap it all into place, check for square and clamp it up.

Doors and Drawers

I used half-blind dovetail joinery for the drawers, using poplar as a secondary wood for the side and backs of the drawers, and ¼" birch plywood for the bottoms. The drawer bottoms slide into ¼" × ¼" grooves cut ½" up on the sides and drawer front. The backs are cut ½" shorter than the sides to allow the bot-

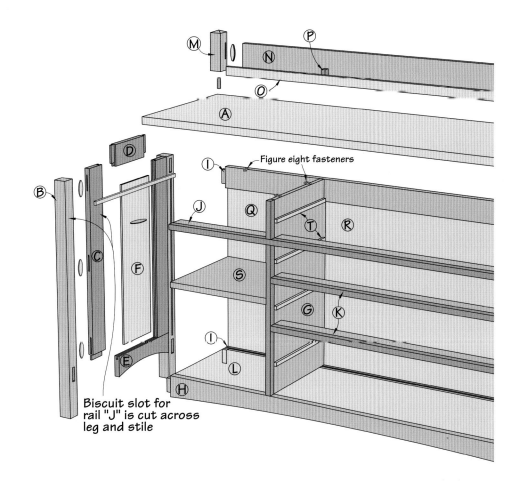

Figure eight fasteners

Biscuit slot for
rail "J" is cut across
leg and stile

tom to slide into place.

I went with a traditional drawer slide method and cut ⅝"-wide by ⁵⁄₁₆"-deep grooves in the drawer sides before assembly. Once the drawer was assembled, I notched the drawer backs to continue the groove the length of the drawer. I then mounted oak drawer runners to the inside of the cabinet. The captured drawer runners (with a little paraffin) prove a fine drawer slide and keep the drawer from drooping when opened to full length. The size and location of your runners is critical and should be checked carefully before mounting.

The doors are built pretty much the same way as the cabinet's side panels, though I used a ¾"-deep groove and tongue for extra strength. I mortised the hinges into the doors only (half the thickness of the hinge), and it provided good spacing for the door in the opening.

Top and Plate Rail
I've included a plate rail on my sideboard that is a traditional touch. How-

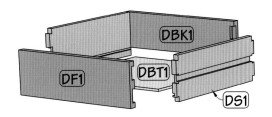

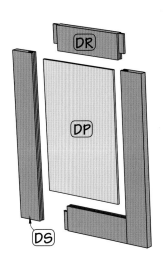

Arches Without a Compass

If you've taken a moment to try to figure out the radius necessary to make the arch on either the side or front rails, you'll know you're looking for a compass with about a 20' beam. Since this is a little silly, here's an easier way:

Find a piece of hardwood fall-off measuring about ¼" x 1" x 72". Tap a couple of brad nails into the rail at the extreme ends of the arch. Then bend the strip from the center up 1" and clamp it in place. Take a pencil and trace the inside of the strip, and there's your arch. Obviously a shorter strip will work just as well for the side rails.

Schedule of Materials: Sideboard

CABINET

No.	Ltr.	Item	Dimensions T W L	Material	Comments
I	A	Top	1" x 19" x 66"	WO	
4	B	Legs	1¾" x 1¾" x 33"	WO	
4	C	Side stiles	1" x 3" x 26½"	WO	½" TOE
2	D	Side rails	1" x 3" x 8"	WO	½" TBE
2	E	Side rails	1" x 3" x 13"	WO	
2	F	Side panels	¼" x 8" x 24"	WO Ply	
2	G	Partitions	¾" x 15¼" x 26"	WO/Ply	
I	H	Front rail	1" x 3" x 61½"	WO	¾" TBE
2	I	Rear rails	1" x 3" x 61½"	Poplar	¾" TBE
I	J	Drawer rail	¾" x 3" x 60"	WO/Ply	
2	K	Drawer rails	¾" x 3" x 28¼"	WO/Ply	
I	L	Bottom	¾" x 13¾" x 60"	Ply	
2	M	Posts	1¾" x 1¾" x 5¾"	WO	20° bevel
I	N	Plate rail	¾" x 3½" x 60"	WO	
I	O	Front rail	⅝" x 1¼" x 63⅛"	WO	45° bevel
2	P	Rail spacers	⅝" x 1" x ⅞"	WO	
2	Q	Backs	¼" x 15⅝" x 24"	WO Ply	
I	R	Back	¼" x 29" x 24"	Plywood	
2	S	Shelves	¾" x 15" x 14"	WO/Ply	
12	T	Runners	⅜" x ½" x 13"	WO	

DOORS & DRAWERS (Sizes allow a 1/16" gap around doors & drawers)

No.	Ltr.	Item	Dimensions T W L	Material	Comments
4	DS	Stiles	¾" x 3" x 20⅛"	WO	
4	DR	Rails	¾" x 3" x 10½"	WO	¾" TBE
2	DP	Panels	¼" x 10½" x 15⅝"	WO Ply	
2	DF1	Fronts	¾" x 4⅞" x 15"	WO	
I	DF2	Front	¾" x 4⅞" x 28⅛"	WO	
6	DS1	Sides	9/16" x 4⅞" x 14"	Poplar	
2	DBK1	Backs	¾" x 4⅜" x 15"	Poplar	
I	DBK2	Back	¾" x 4⅜" x 28⅛"	Poplar	
I	DF3	Front	¾" x 5½" x 28⅛"	WO	
2	DS3	Sides	9/16" x 5½" x 14"	Poplar	
I	DBK3	Back	¾" x 5" x 28⅛"	Poplar	
I	DF4	Front	¾" x 5⅞" x 28⅛"	WO	
2	DS4	Sides	9/16" x 5⅞" x 14"	Poplar	
I	DBK4	Back	¾" x 5⅜" x 28⅛"	Poplar	
I	DF5	Front	¾" x 7" x 28⅛"	WO	
2	DS5	Sides	9/16" x 7" x 14"	Poplar	
I	DBK5	Back	¾" x 6½" x 28⅛"	Poplar	
2	DBT1	Bottoms	¼" x 14⅛" x 14 5/16"	Ply	
4	DBT2	Bottoms	¼" x 14⅛" x 27 7/16"	Ply	

WO = white oak • WO/Ply = white oak plywood • TOE = tenon on one end • TBE = tenon on both ends

ever, you may opt to leave it off. The plate rail piece is biscuited between the two posts, while the front rail is nailed in place to the front of the posts (see diagram). I used a 23-gauge air pinner that left almost no hole to putty.

The two post tops are beveled on four sides to a 20-degree angle to form a "point." I did this on the table saw with a stop mounted on the miter gauge. Four quick cuts and you're done. With the plate rail assembled, mark the drilling location on the top and drill the dowel holes in the top, but leave the rail loose until after applying the finish.

Attach the top using figure-eight fasteners. They require very little space and allow the top to move during changes in humidity. The last pieces to cut are the backs and the shelves for the door sections.

Hardware and Finish

Now mount the hardware. The pulls shown are impressive, and they should be. The pulls are Stickley reproductions and priced at $30 each. While they're worth the money, you may choose to use more affordable pulls.

Finishing an Arts and Crafts piece is always a challenge. The trick is to get the right color and still get the ray flake to "pop" from the wood. Start by applying an alcohol-soluble aniline dye. Many colors are available, but choose one with a reddish-brown cast, such as a brown mahogany. Because it's alcohol based,

this dye will dry quickly and can soon be recoated with a warm brown glaze. While wiping the excess glaze from the piece you can control how dark the finish will be. After allowing the glaze to dry overnight, the final step is a couple of coats of satin lacquer. If you use shellac or varnish, be careful as the alcohol carrier can allow the stain to run.

This is an impressive piece, and I'm pleased with its scaled-down proportions. There's only one drawback to building your own Arts and Crafts sideboard: The next logical step is a dining table and chairs. Maybe next year.

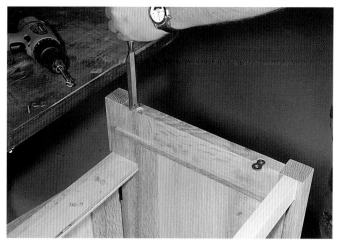

Use a Forstner bit to recess the smaller end of the fasteners into the top edge of the partitions and side panels. Then take a chisel and notch the inner half of the recess to form a V, which will allow the fastener to swivel front to back. This allows for wood movement and will keep the solid top from pulling the cabinet apart.

With everything ready to finish, there's something satisfying in seeing the drawer dovetails surrounded by great hardware. If you want to keep the dovetails highly visible, carefully tape off the sides of the drawers before staining.

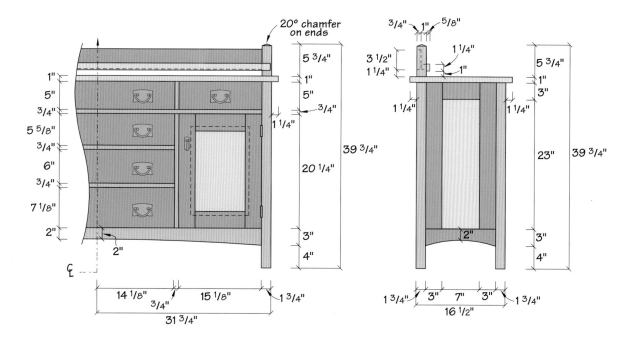

SOURCES

From Rockler Woodworking
(800) 279-4441, or www.rockler.com
10 - #62943 Stickley V-pulls - $29.99 ea.
 2 - #26815 Vertical pulls - $17.99 ea.
 2 - pr #27979 Stickley hinges - $6.99 ea.
Desk top fasteners #21650 - $3.99 for a
pack of eight

Economy Option: Woodcraft
(800) 225-1153
10 - #123874 Mission pulls - $9.99 ea.
 2 - #123876 Vertical pulls - $5.99 ea.
Use the same hinges.

Perfect for dropping off your keys on the way in and checking your appearance on the way out.

Wright Hall Tree

You may be asking what Frank Lloyd Wright is doing in an Arts and Crafts furniture book. Actually the Arts and Crafts movement owes a debt to Wright for his forward-thinking Prairie-style home designs. When Wright conceived the Prarie style, he designed the house as well as the furnishings and often the silverware and the appropriate dress for the homeowner. Wright developed a line of Prairie furniture that echoes the Arts and Crafts influences of simplicity, honest construction and only having things in your home that you considered beautiful. When the home owner could not afford to have Wright design their furniture, he often told them that furniture from Gustav Stickley would be okay.

Stickley went on to include a Prairie style line of furniture patterned on Wright's designs and today these pieces fetch a great price. Though the hall tree we've shown here was not designed by Wright or Stickley, it does use an architectural detail found in Wright's office added to his Oak Park, Illinois residence in 1895. The triple-banded column with top cap also appears in work designed by Wright for the Dana Thomas house and other Wright locations. The banding appears as a distinctive design in much of his Prairie-style work, and the cantilevered shelf also echoes much of his work of the period.

Construction

Construction of this hall tree is very simple with one minor exception – the quadrilinear posts. Used first as a construction technique by Leopold Stickley, the idea is to use four pieces with quarter-sawn faces to form a post so each face of the post shows the ray flake. While simply mitering the long edges of the piece to form the post would work, it's difficult to hold the miters tight and accurate on each corner during glue-up. Leopold solved this by making an interlocking joint at the miter that helped position the miter, and added extra strength. Today the lock-miter router bit has made the quadrilinear post easily accessible to any woodworker.

Start construction by ripping the eight pieces to form the sides of the two posts. Set up a router table with a lock miter bit (see photo 1). On each post, two of the sides will be run through the bit lying flat, good face up. The adjoining two sides will be run on edge with the inner face against the fence. Before running the actual pieces, run some test pieces to adjust the cut. By adjusting the bit up or down, and adjusting the fence location, you will be able to make a nearly invisible, knife-edge miter. Depending on the size of the router in your table, it may be advisable to cut the lock-miter joints in two passes of increasing depth. Whether one or two cuts, use fingerboards and hold-downs to keep the side tight against the router bit. If the piece moves away from the bit during the cut, the miter will not close tight, and the piece will need to be re run. Go ahead

and run all the post sides.

With the miters cut, glue-up is pretty simple, and more tidy than normal. By running a bead of glue into the groove formed by the bit, the glue squeeze-out to the outside of the post is minimal. In addition, the lock miter allows you to use only a half-dozen clamps to glue up the posts, where a standard mitered post would require dozens of clamps.

Let the posts dry while you head back to the saw to cut the pieces for the upper and lower mirror supports, the shelf and the base. The mirror supports are two pieces glued together in a long-grain joint to form a "T". Clamp these up with the 1¼"-wide piece on edge, centered on the 1¾" piece. Throughout this piece, I took advantage of a 23-gauge, headless micro-pinner. The pinner leaves an almost invisible hole in the wood and provides strength while the glue dries. You can add a few headless pins to the mirror supports to hold them in place while they dry.

The shelf and base are mitered frames held together by biscuits at the corners. One difference is that the shelf has a ½" × ½" groove run ½" down on the inside face of each piece. This groove will capture the piece to form the shelf surface. Cut the grooves in the shelf frame piece using the table saw with a dado stack, by adjusting the cut using a regular saw blade, or by using a router with edge guide and an up spiral router bit.

With the grooves cut, prepare the

1 *The finished post shows the inter-locking pattern on the lock miter joints. The lock miter bit is shown in the router table.*

2 *If ever there was an invaluable tool that was amazingly cheap, it's dowel centers. Costing less than $5, a set of dowel centers allows you to unerringly locate a dowel joint with very simple tools. Here the dowel centers are used to locate the placement of the mirror supports.*

11" × 15" shelf surface. If you need to glue up this piece, plan your joint so that it falls in the center of the piece and provides an attractive matched pattern. Go ahead and cut the biscuit slots, then glue up the two frames. Place the shelf piece in the groove, but don't use glue on the groove. The shelf should have ⅛" space all the way around to allow the solid wood shelf room to ex-

pand during atmospheric changes.

The next step is to carefully locate the positions for attaching the two mirror supports, the shelf and the base. Use the diagrams to determine the correct locations, and mark them on the inside faces of the two posts. The mirror supports are attached to the posts with ⅜" dowels. The shelf is screwed and glued in place from the underside

of the shelf, while the base can be dow-eled in place, or can be glued and screwed, with the screw heads recessed and plugged.

Drill the two dowel holes into the ends of each mirror support. Then use dowel centers, placed in the dowel holes, to locate the supports centered on the post faces. With the locations de-termined, drill the holes into the posts. If you're doweling the base into the posts, use the same process as above to locate the dowels for the base frame. Locate the base frame extending 1" be-yond the rear surface of the posts.

Glue the hall tree together, clamping across the assembly at the mirror sup-ports and the base. If you aren't dowel-ing the base frame, still go ahead and glue and screw the base frame in place at this time to help stabilize the assem-bly. Make sure the base frame is square to the posts, or the hall tree will lean too far forward or back.

When the hall tree assembly has dried, drill clearance holes in the shelf sides to attach the shelf flush to the back edge of the posts. The shelf is lo-cated 36" up from the floor. I find this a good standing surface height, but you may want to adjust the shelf height to best fit you comfort level. Attach the

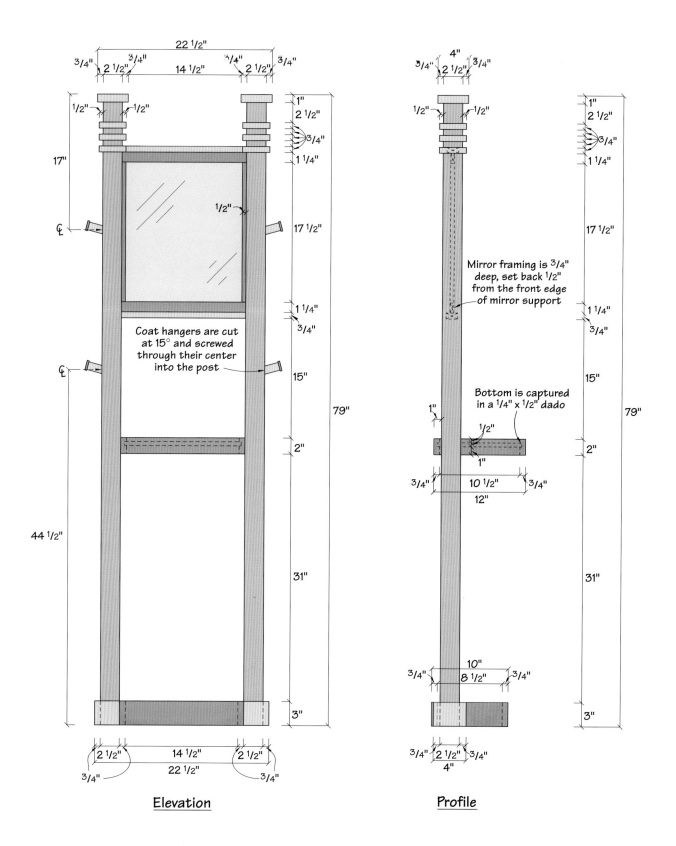

Mirror framing is 3/4"
deep, set back 1/2"
from the front edge
of mirror support

Coat hangers are cut
at 15° and screwed
through their center
into the post

Bottom is captured
in a 1/4" x 1/2" dado

Elevation

Profile

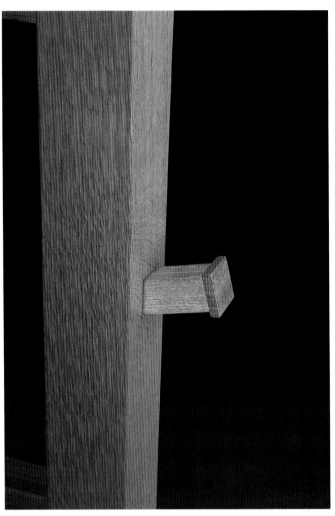

3 With the hall tree assembled, the banding details and caps are added. On the top left band the hole made by the micro pinner is on the left, while a hole made by a nail set is on the right. My preference is easy.

4 When you pin the caps onto the coat hangers, make sure you locate the pins to avoid the screw in the center. The thin pins are easily redirected by the grain of the wood, and hitting a screw could easily cause the pin to blow out the side of the hook.

Schedule of Materials: Wright Hall Tree

No.	Lett.	Item	Dimensions T W L	Material
8	A	Post sides	$^3/_4$" x $2^1/_2$" x 78"	White oak
2	B	Mirror supports	$^3/_4$" x $1^3/_4$" x 16"	White oak
2	C	Mirror supports	$^3/_4$" x $1^1/_4$" x 16"	White oak
2	D	Shelf front and back	$^3/_4$" x 2" x 16"	White oak
2	E	Shelf sides	$^3/_4$" x 2" x 12"	White oak
I	F	Shelf	$^1/_2$" x 11" x 15"	White oak
2	G	Base front and back	$^3/_4$" x 3" x 16"	White oak
2	H	Base sides	$^3/_4$" x 3" x 10"	White oak
22	I	Band mouldings	$^1/_2$" x $^3/_4$" x $3^1/_2$"	White oak
4	J	Band mouldings	$^1/_2$" x $^3/_4$" x 1"	White oak
2	K	Mirror stops	$^1/_2$" x $^3/_4$" x $17^1/_2$"	White oak
2	L	Post caps	1" x 4" x 4"	White oak
4	M	Coat hangers	1" x 1" x 2"	White oak
4	N	Hanger caps	$^1/_4$" x $1^1/_4$" x $1^1/_4$"	White oak
4	O	Base mouldings	$^3/_4$" x 3" x $3^1/_4$"	White oak
2	P	Base mouldings	$^3/_4$" x 3" x 4"	White oak
I	Q	Back	$^1/_4$" x 16" x 20"	White oak

shelf (again using glue), and check for square to the posts.

The next step is to cut and attach the decorative banding, base and post caps. Run out a couple of lengths of $^1/_2$" × $^3/_4$" strips. While you should be able to cut all 22 of the mitered bands to length, I've yet to find a mitering job that didn't require some fitting. Because of this I individually fit each of the $3^1/_2$" pieces. Start with the lower band, aligning it with the top edge of the upper mirror support. I applied a couple of dabs of glue to each piece and tacked it in place using the micro pinner. Cut and miter the four 1" pieces to fit on the inside faces against the mirror support.

With the lower detail in place, use a scrap $^1/_2$" × $^3/_4$" piece to space between the next two levels. When all the banding is in place, cut the 1" × 4" × 4" caps and glue and nail them in place into the posts from the top. Since you're pretty good at mitering now, cut the 3" pieces to wrap the base of each post, in line with the base frame. Two last pieces of moulding to attach are the vertical mirror stops. Cut them to size and fit them for length between the upper and lower mirror supports, then glue them in place.

The next step is to cut and attach the coat hooks. Cut the four 1" × 1" piece to 2" length, cutting one end of each at a 15-degree angle. Next set up your drill press with a ³⁄₁₆" bit and set up a fence and stop to allow you to drill down through the center of each piece, starting the hole from the angled end. Drill the hole all the way through the piece. Then chuck a ⅜" bit into a cordless drill and drill from the square end of the piece into the existing hole to form a countersink ¼" deep.

Determine the location of the hooks on the posts, and use a ⅛" bit to start a pilot hole in the post. To drill the pilot hole at the proper angle, slide the coat hook over the drill bit and align the angle by sight as you drill. Attach the coat hooks to the posts using 2½" screws, allowing the head of the screw to recess into the countersink hole. To hide the screw hole and finish off the coat hooks, cut the ¼" × 1¼" × 1¼" caps and glue and tack them in place, again using the micro pinner.

Wright is one of the few Arts and Crafts designers that used a lighter finish on many of his pieces. Because of this I opted to leave the hall tree almost natural. To give the white oak a slightly aged look I used a wiping varnish to wipe down the entire piece, then applied a couple of coats of a satin finish clear lacquer.

The last step is to fit the mirror and the ¼" mirror backer and put the mirror in place. I used glazing points to hold the mirror and backer in place. This hall tree not only provides a great place to hang your jacket, but the shelf is amazingly useful for tossing keys, glasses and all the other stuff we drag into our houses that we can never find when we try and leave the house.

5 The base moulding doesn't really add any stability, but it does finish off the look of the base nicely.

Learn the most essential joint for building Arts and Crafts furniture as you construct these two frames.

Two Frames

IF YOU'RE NEW TO WOODWORKING OR TO ARTS AND CRAFTS FURNITURE, you should try your hand at building a frame for a picture or mirror first. You'll learn how to cut a mortise-and-tenon joint without the fear of blowing an entire Morris chair. You'll learn how to peg this joint to make it even more durable. And you'll get a feel for working with white oak and get to experiment with finishes.

The picture frame featured here was built to hold a photo in a mat that measures 16" × 20", which is a pretty standard size. It's a simple matter to adjust the measurements of the stiles and rails if your photo or painting is bigger. I built this frame after a visit to the Gamble House in Pasadena, California,

which was designed by the Greene brothers. On the tour of the house it became evident that one of the keys to their designs was that everything be in threes: three rails, three cutouts, three inlays. So with that in mind, I designed this traditional Arts and Crafts frame.

The second piece is a mirror frame designed to hold a standard 24" × 24" mirror, which is available at most home center stores for about $20. This design was taken from an actual mirror that was featured at an auction held by Treadway Gallery of Cincinnati, Ohio. Construction of both frames is similar, but because they use different thicknesses of wood, I'll cover each one separately.

Picture Frame

The first step is to choose your wood. With picture frames you have to remember that you've got only a few sticks of wood so you want to show the best grain possible. However, that being said, you also don't want the grain to be so wild that it competes with or outshines the artwork it's supposed to display. So look for ray flake that is somewhere in the middle.

Cut all your pieces to size and get ready to cut your mortise-and-tenon joints. The rule of thumb is to cut your tenons to be half as thick as your wood. So if your wood is ¾" thick, your tenons should be ⅜" thick. For wood this narrow, you should cut ¼" shoulders on the edges. I usually make all my tenons 1" long. So the tenons on the rails should measure ⅜" thick, 1½" wide and 1" long. I like to cut my tenons using a dado stack in a table saw. For more on this technique, you can read the chapter about the Shop of the Crafters Morris Chair, which begins on page 18.

Now cut your mortises. You want your mortises to be a little deeper than your tenons so the tenon won't bottom out in your mortise. So your mortises should measure ⅜" thick, 1½" wide and 1¹⁄₁₆" long. I like to use a hollow chisel mortiser, but it's not necessary. If you own a drill press you can cut these mortises using a ⅜" Forstner bit and a fence clamped to your drill press' table. Then square the corners using a chisel.

While you're set up for mortising, make the three square cutouts on the bottom rail.

Now cut the ¼"-deep by ½"-wide rabbet on the backs of the stiles and rails to hold the mirror in place. You'll have to stop the rabbet in the stiles, but this is a simple thing to do with a rabbeting bit in a router table.

Now test the fit of everything and clamp up your frame without glue to make sure everything fits and closes tightly. When you're satisfied, put glue in the mortises and clamp up your picture frame. Make sure your frame is square by measuring the frame's diagonals (from corner to corner). If the diagonal measurements are not identical, place a clamp across the two corners that were longer. Apply a slight bit of pressure and check your diagonals again.

When the glue is dry, remove the frame from the clamps. Now peg your tenons for additional strength. I like to use ¼" oak dowels. The size of store-bought dowels is rarely consistent, so first cut some holes in scrap pieces of wood to test out how your dowels fit. I like to use a drill press for this operation. When you've found the perfect bit, drill the holes about ⅝" deep into your frame. The holes don't need to go all the way through. Put a little glue into the hole and hammer the dowel home. Cut any excess flush to the stiles.

Now finish sand the frame. Start with 100-grit, then move up to 120 and finish with 150. This frame is finished with a simple mahogany gel stain. After your stain dries, cover it with three coats of a clear finish. Install the glass, photo and mat, and hold them in the rabbet using mirror clips, which screw to the back side of your frame.

Mirror Frame

This frame is a little more work, but the operations are all the same. After you cut your pieces to size, cut your tenons on the ends of the stiles. Because this stock is ⅞" thick, you'll need to make your tenons ⁷⁄₁₆" thick. So your tenons should measure ⁷⁄₁₆" thick, 2" wide and 1" long. Your mortises should be ⁷⁄₁₆" thick, 2" wide and 1¹⁄₁₆" long. Once you've got your joints cut, turn your attention to the top rail.

The top rail slopes from 4" high in the middle to 3" on the ends. Mark this on the rail and make the cut on a band saw. Clean up the cut on your jointer.

Now cut the rabbet on the back of the pieces to hold the mirror in place. I cut a ⅛"-deep by ¼"-wide rabbet using a rabbeting bit in a router table.

Test the fit of all your joints and then glue up your frame. When the glue is dry, peg the joints. Cut out the two corbels according to the pattern in the diagram and finish sand all your parts. Glue the corbels in place (flush to the back side of the frame) and finish the frame.

I combined two dyes to get this dark color — a brown dye and a deep red dye. Then I followed it with three coats of a clear finish.

When the finish is dry, put the mirror in its rabbet and use mirror clips to hold it in place.

Schedule of Materials: Arts and Crafts Picture Frame

No.	Item	Dimensions T W L	Comments
2	Stiles	¾" x 3" x 26⅛"	
3	Rails	¾" x 2" x 21⅛"	1" TBE

Schedule of Materials: Arts and Crafts Mirror Frame

No.	Item	Dimensions T W L	Comments
1	Top rail	⅞" x 4" x 33½"	
1	Bot. rail	⅞" x 2½" x 30½"	
2	Stiles	⅞" x 2½" x 25½"	1" TBE
2	Corbels	¾" x 2¼" x 5"	

TBE=tenon on both ends

Picture Frame

$3/8$" x $1 1/2$" x 1" tenon on both ends

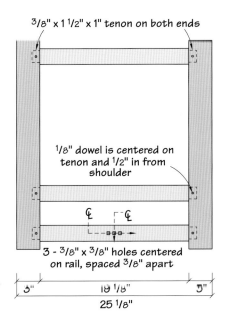

$1/8$" dowel is centered on tenon and $1/2$" in from shoulder

℄   ℄

3 - $3/8$" x $3/8$" holes centered on rail, spaced $3/8$" apart

3"   18 1/8"   5"

25 1/8"

Detail of rabbet

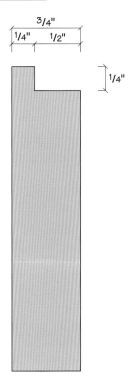

3/4"

1/4"   1/2"

1/4"

Mirror Frame Corbel Detail

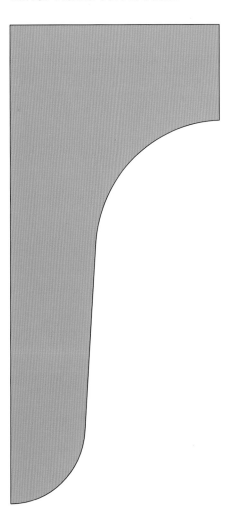

Mirror Frame

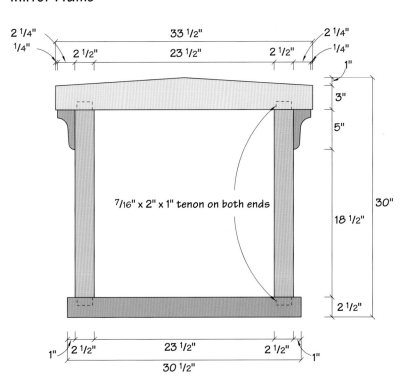

2 1/4"   33 1/2"   2 1/4"

1/4"   2 1/2"   23 1/2"   2 1/2"   1/4"

1"

3"

5"

$7/16$" x 2" x 1" tenon on both ends

18 1/2"

30"

2 1/2"

1"   2 1/2"   23 1/2"   2 1/2"   1"

30 1/2"

**Make this turn-of-the-century place for your spirits or
(for teetotalers) an eye-catching small desk.**

Cellarette

A LOT OF THE LITERATURE ABOUT THE ARTS AND CRAFTS MOVEMENT gives the impression that its followers were serious folks. Some devotees even lived in communes dedicated to philosophy, the arts and producing beautiful objects.

But that doesn't mean our turn-of-the-century ancestors didn't know how to party. Almost all major manufacturers of Arts and Crafts furniture featured cellarettes (also called liquor cabinets) in their catalogs. Some companies, such as the Shop of the Crafters in Cincinnati, Ohio, even built their reputation on selling a wide variety of cellarettes.

Now I know that not everybody drinks. In fact, I drink hard liquor so rarely this project seemed impractical for my home, but my wife insisted. So to make this project appropriate for every home, I made the dimensions so it can also work perfectly as a drop-front desk. If you build it as a desk, my only recommendation would be to make it more stable by either making the base 2" deeper at the bottom or attaching the desk to your wall. The drop front is sturdy as is; but these extra measures will ensure your desk never topples.

Construction is straightforward. Mortise the two shelves into the sides. Biscuit the rails into the sides. Screw the top to the base with cleats. Attach the drop front with hinges.

Begin by cutting all pieces to size. Lay out the locations of the shelves and rails on the sides according to the diagram. Cut the ⅜"-deep by ½"-wide mor-

Schedule of Materials: Cellarette

BASE PARTS

No.	Item	Dimensions T W L	Material	Notes
2	Sides	$3/4$" x 12" x 47"	Oak	tapers to 10" at top
1	Top	$3/4$" x $11\frac{1}{2}$" x 40"	Oak	$3/8$" x 1" chamfer on bottom
1	Middle shelf	$3/4$" x 9" x $30\frac{3}{4}$"	Oak	$1/2$" x $3/8$" tenon both ends
1	Bookshelf	$3/4$" x 8" x $30\frac{3}{4}$"	Oak	$1/2$" x $3/8$" tenon both ends
1	Book rail	$3/4$" x 2" x 30"	Oak	biscuited into sides
2	Top rails	$3/4$" x 2" x 30"	Oak	biscuited into sides
4	Corbels	$3/4$" x $1\frac{3}{4}$" x 6"	Oak	glued to sides
4	Cleats	$3/4$" x $3/4$" x 6"	Oak	screwed to sides and top
1	Back	$1/4$" x $17\frac{1}{2}$" x 31"	Oak ply	in $1/4$" x $1/2$" rabbet in back

DROP-FRONT PARTS

No.	Item	Dimensions T W L	Material	Notes
2	Stiles	$3/4$" x $3\frac{1}{2}$" x 17"	Oak	$1/4$" x $3/4$" groove inside
1	Top rail	$3/4$" x 5" x $24\frac{1}{2}$"	Oak	groove bottom • $1/4$" x $3/4$" tenons on ends
1	Bottom rail	$3/4$" x 2" x $24\frac{1}{2}$"	Oak	groove top • $1/4$" x $3/4$" tenons on ends
2	Interior stiles	$3/4$" x $3\frac{1}{4}$" x $11\frac{1}{2}$"	Oak	groove sides • $1/4$" x $3/4$" tenons on ends
3	Panels	$1/2$" x $6\frac{1}{2}$" x 11"	Oak	$1/4$" x $1/2$" rabbet on back

tises for the middle shelf and the book-shelf. Then cut the tenons on the shelves to fit.

Cut the taper on the front of the sides. The taper begins 6" up from the bottom and ends where the top is 10" wide. Sand all the base parts.

Cut slots for the biscuits in the rails and sides. Now glue up the base and clamp. When it's dry, use a router and a rabbeting bit to cut the $1/4$"-deep by $1/2$"-rabbet in the back of the sides to hold the back. The top back rail and the middle shelf also hold the back in place. Cut the back to fit. Cut the corbels to size and attach with glue.

Build the drop front. Cut a $1/4$"-wide by $3/4$" groove on the inside edges of the rails and exterior stiles. Cut the same groove on both long edges of the two interior stiles. Then cut the $1/4$" $\times$ $3/4$" tenons on the ends of the two rails and on the top and bottom of the two interior stiles. Now cut the panels to size and cut a $1/4$" by $1/2$"-wide rabbet on the back of the panels. Apply glue to the tenons (not the panels), clamp and allow to dry.

Mortise the hinges into the middle shelf and the drop front. Attach the chains to the sides and drop front. Add magnets, magnetic catches or a lock to hold the drop front in place. Center the pull on the top rail and attach it.

Cut the top to size. Cut a $3/8$" $\times$ 1" chamfer on the underside of the sides and front of the top using your table

saw. Drill clearance holes in the cleats. Attach the four cleats to the sides and rails, then screw the base to the top through these cleats.

Disassemble and sand. I used a warm brown glaze and two coats of lacquer

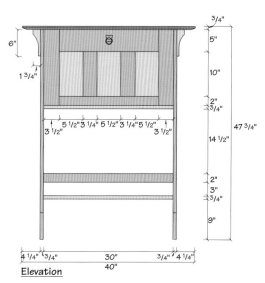

Plan

Elevation

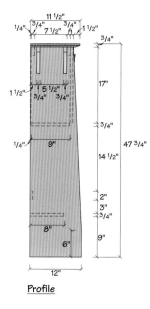

Profile

Aging Your Hardware With 'Gun Blue'

Steel hardware can be easily aged by dipping it in gun blue (available at most gun stores) for a minute or two. I've also found that brass hardware can be aged using this chemical. First remove the lacquer from the hardware with lacquer thinner, sanding or both. Dip it in gun blue, remove it when black and then coat the hardware with lacquer.

SUPPLIES

2 - Hinges
Paxton Hardware
(800) 241-9741 or
www.paxtonhardware.com
Item # 4100 • call for price

1 - Pull
Horton Brasses
(860) 635-4400 or
www.horton-brasses.com
Item # MS-13 • call for price

Lee Valley Tools
(800) 871-8158 or
www.leevalley.com
2 - Chains • $4.75 each

for the finish. I aged the brass hardware by soaking the parts in gun blue for 30 seconds. Let the metal parts dry and then give them a coat of lacquer. Attach the drop front and top to the base. Nail the back into place. Cheers.

Limbert Wastepaper Box

CHARLES P. LIMBERT'S FURNITURE DESIGNS are best thought of as American Arts and Crafts pieces that went to finishing school in Europe. Like no other furniture maker of his time, Limbert was able to combine the massive straight forms of American pieces from the Stickleys and progressive design from Europe. The result is straightforward furniture that has a certain flair to it, a subtle curve or a cutout.

This wastebasket is a replica of the #255 Wastepaper Box found in Booklet No. 112, one of the many catalogs his company produced after the turn of the century. The proportions of this can are identical to the original. The joinery is simple and sturdy, much like that I've seen on other Limbert pieces. The only change I've made in the appearance is that I used cherry instead of quarter-sawn white oak.

This project can be built with a table saw, a router and a few hand tools. Construction is straightforward. The panels are glued into ⅛"-deep grooves in the corner posts. The bottom is screwed to the sides through cleats. Begin by gluing up any panels you'll need for the sides and trimming all the other parts to size. When your panels are ready, cut out the handle and the small lift on the bottom of each. I did this by first making a plywood template of the cutout and arch. I shaped the template using a jigsaw and cleaned up the cuts with a rasp and sandpaper. Then I used a pattern-cutting bit in my router to cut the

Patching Trick

Checks in your boards can be tricky. They might get larger, they might not. To fill mine, I made a quick and effective putty. The putty is made from equal parts of fine cherry sawdust and cyanoacrylate glue (superglue to most people). The putty sets up in about five minutes as hard as a rock. It's sandable and — when finished — looks like one of those dark streaks of cherry that's common to the species. Then cross your fingers and hope the check stays small. Be sure to have some solvent on hand if you mess up the patch.

two shapes. When your panels are done, turn your attention to the posts.

The most important aspect of the posts is to make sure you center the ⅛"-deep by ½"-wide groove that receives the panel. I made the cuts using a dado stack in my table saw and squared up the end at the top with a chisel. When your posts are milled, sand everything and begin assembly. The best way to go about this is to first glue up two side assemblies that have two posts and a side piece. When those are dry, glue the two remaining sides into the assemblies and clamp.

Now attach the bottom. When you screw the cleats to the sides and to the bottom piece, be sure to make the screw holes in the cleats in the shape of an elongated oval. This will allow for wood movement. Disassemble everything and then finish. I used Moser's Light Sheraton Mahogany dye, available from Woodworkers Supply (800) 645-9292, item #W13304, $11.90 for four ounces of powder. Then I added a coat of clear finish, sanded it and applied a coat of warm brown glaze, which is available at professional paint stores. After allowing that to dry overnight, I added two more coats of a clear finish.

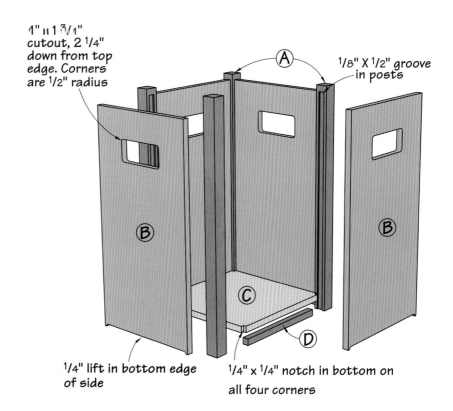

1" ıı 1 ¾" cutout, 2 ¼" down from top edge. Corners are ½" radius

⅛" X ½" groove in posts

¼" lift in bottom edge of side

¼" x ¼" notch in bottom on all four corners

Schedule of Materials: Limbert Wastepaper Box

No.	Lett.	Item	Dimensions T W L	Material
4	A	Posts	1" x 1" x 18"	Cherry
4	B	Sides	1" x 1" x 18"	Cherry
1	C	Bottom	1" x 1" x 18"	Cherry
2	D	Cleats	1" x 1" x 18"	Cherry

Garden Storage Bench

OUTDOOR ARTS AND CRAFTS FURNITURE was almost always made from wicker or hickory sticks, so when it came to designing a garden bench in that style I had almost no examples to turn to. However, after collecting and building this type of furniture for almost a decade, I knew one thing had to be true: It would have to be built to last.

Fact is, I could have glued and screwed this whole thing together in a few hours. But because this bench was built for my sister-in-law as a gift for her new home (and because I don't want to be haunted by the ghost of Gustav Stickley), I decided to take the most traditional approach I could. That meant pegged mortise-and-tenon joints.

All Tenons, All the Time

Begin by cutting all your parts to size and laying out the ½"-thick by 2"-wide by 1"-long mortises on the four legs. Each 7¼"-wide slat in the lower case gets four tenons; that's two on each end. If I'd put only one wide tenon on each end, I would have had to remove too much material in the legs for the mortises. The detail drawing on page 122 shows you how the mortises and tenons are spaced. Now cut your mortises. You'll notice that the mortises on the two adjacent sides meet in the middle of the leg. This means you'll have to miter your tenons on down the road.

Now lay out and cut the through-mortises on the back legs. The through-mortises for the top rail measure

½"-thick by 5¼"-wide. The through-mortises for the bottom rail measure ½" thick by 2" wide. Now cut your tenons and miter the ones for the lower case. To clean out the area between the two tenons on the lower case pieces, use a backsaw and a coping saw.

Cut the 2" arches on the front, sides and back pieces using a band saw. Clean up your work with sandpaper. Now locate where the center seat support will go and cut biscuit slots to hold it in place. Sand everything to 150-grit.

Assembly

After first dry assembling your bench, glue up the bench in stages. First glue up the front pieces between the front legs and the back pieces between the back legs. I recommend polyurethane glue here for two reasons. One, it's quite weather-resistant; and two, it has a long open time, which helps with this glue-up. Put glue in the mortises only, and be stingy. You don't want a lot of foamy squeeze-out. After the glue has cured, glue the side pieces and center seat support between the front and back leg assemblies.

Screw the two slat support pieces to the inside of the frame (one on the front, one on the back). Then screw the eight slats to the supports with about 2½" between each slat. Once that's done, peg all the mortises. I used ¼" × ¼" × 1¼" strips of walnut. First drill a ¼" hole that's 1⅛" deep. Carve the walnut strips round on one end, then hammer

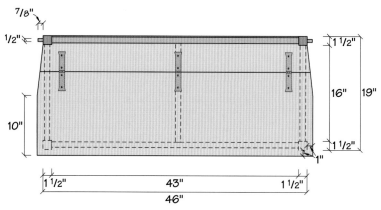

them home. Cut the waste flush.

Now work on the seat. Notch the rear seat piece around the legs. Attach it to the frame using cleats and screws. Then attach the front seat piece to the rear seat piece using the hand-forged hinges from Lee Valley. These are rustic, inexpensive but of excellent quality. You'll need to scare up some equally rustic screws to attach the hinges. I used some old no. 7 × 1" flathead screws.

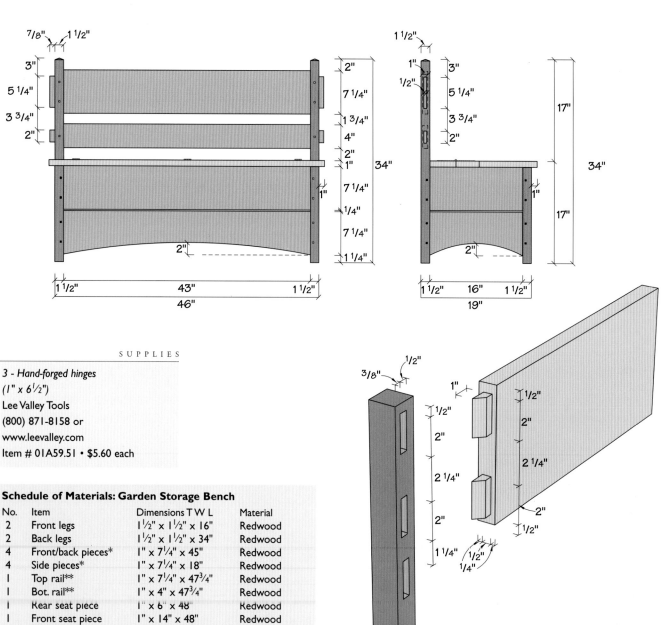

SUPPLIES

*3 - Hand-forged hinges
(1" x 6½")*
Lee Valley Tools
(800) 871-8158 or
www.leevalley.com
Item # 01A59.51 • $5.60 each

Schedule of Materials: Garden Storage Bench

No.	Item	Dimensions T W L	Material
2	Front legs	1½" x 1½" x 16"	Redwood
2	Back legs	1½" x 1½" x 34"	Redwood
4	Front/back pieces*	1" x 7¼" x 45"	Redwood
4	Side pieces*	1" x 7¼" x 18"	Redwood
1	Top rail**	1" x 7¼" x 47¾"	Redwood
1	Bot. rail**	1" x 4" x 47¾"	Redwood
1	Rear seat piece	1" x 6" x 48"	Redwood
1	Front seat piece	1" x 14" x 48"	Redwood
1	Seat support	1" x 3" x 16¾"	Redwood
2	Slat supports	1½" x 1½" x 42"	Cedar
8	Slats	¾" x 3" x 16¾"	Cedar

* 1" mitered tenon on both ends, included in measurement
** 2⅜" through-tenon on both ends, included in measurement

What is Quarter-sawing?

Quarter-sawing is the practice of first cutting a log into quarters and then cutting the resulting pie-shaped wedges into boards. When a quarter-sawn board is examined from the end, the annular rings will run 45 to 90 degrees to the face. This results in a board with extraordinary stability. Boards with ring angles between 45 and 80 degrees are known as rift cuts and those with angles between 80 and 90 degrees are fully quarter-sawn.

Quarter-sawn oak was, and still is, the wood of choice for Stickley pieces. When oak is quarter-sawn, its medullary rays (tissues radiating from the pith of a tree trunk that intersect the growth rings and carry sap) yield a unique decorative pattern with exposed rays known as flakes.

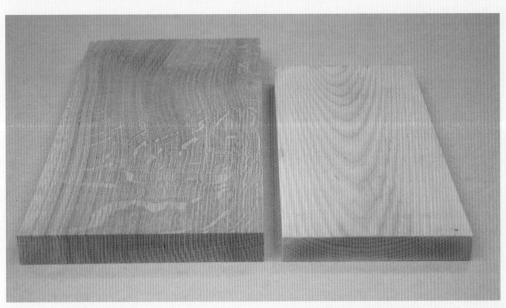

Quarter-sawn oak (on the left) has nearly vertical end grain. Flat-sawn wood (on the right) has less-than-45-degree end grain.

How to Even Lumber

1. Crosscut your board to about 1" longer than you want the finished board to be.

2. Now you'll cut a straight edge. Using a chalk line or a straight edge, mark a straight line about $1/2$" wider than the final dimension down the length of the board. Then rip the lumber freehand with a band saw.

3. Next, surface one face of your board. Using push blocks, pass one face of the board over a jointer, making shallow cuts with each pass until the face is flat.

4. Place the new flat face against the jointer face and feed the ripped edge over the cutterhead so as to smooth out any flaws. Now you should have a right angle between the faced sides.

5. Now you'll plane the board. Place the flat side of the board face down in a planer and feed the board through. Plane down both sides of the board until you get the thickness you want. If you are going to finish sand later, remember to leave some extra material.

6. To cut your board to the finished width, use a table saw equipped with a rip fence. Place the jointed edge next to the rip fence and rip to the width you want, leaving an extra $1/16$". Pass the board over the jointer to remove the excess material for a smoother surface.

7. For the last step, you'll cut your board to the finished length. Holding a miter gage firmly against the jointed edge of the board, pass the board through the blade enough to square off one end. Now turn the board around to the other end and cut to the final length. You may want to use a miter gage clamp for extra support if you're cutting large boards.

suggested reading

The 1912 and 1915 Gustav Stickley Furniture Catalogs by Gustav Stickley, Mineola, NY: The Athenaeum of Philadelphia/Dover, Dover Publications, 1991.

The 1912 Quaint Furniture Catalogue, Stickley Brothers Company, Grand Rapids, Michigan, edited by Peter and Janet Copeland, New York, New York: Turn of the Century Editions, 1981.

American Bungalow, published quarterly, 123 S. Baldwin Avenue, Sierra Madre, CA 91024, www.ambungalow.com.

American Bungalow Style by Robert Winter and Alexander Vertikoff, with a foreward by John Brinkman, Simon & Schuster, 1996.

Arts & Crafts Furniture: The Complete Brooks Catalog of 1912 by the Brooks Manufacturing Company, Dover Publications, 1993.

Arts & Crafts Furniture, Shop of the Crafters at Cincinnati, edited by Stephen Gray, introduction by Kenneth R. Trapp, New York, New York: Turn of the Century Editions, 1983.

Arts & Crafts: Style and Spirit by Chase Reynolds Ewald, Gibbs Smith, 1999.

Arts & Crafts: The California Home by Douglas Congdon-Martin, Schiffer Publishing, 1998.

Collected Works of Gustav Stickley, edited by Stephen Gray and Robert Edwards, Turn of the Century Editions, 1989.

The Encylopedia of Arts and Crafts by Wendy Kaplan, Knickerbocker Press, 1998.

Frank Lloyd Wright's Furnishings by Carla Lind, Pomegranate, 1995.

Furniture of the American Arts and Crafts Movement by David M. Cathers. Turn of the Century Editions, 1996.

Greene & Greene: Furniture and Related Design by Randell Makinson, Gibbs Smith, 1979.

Greene & Greene Masterworks by Bruce Smith and Alexander Vertikoff, Chronicle Books, 1998.

Greene & Greene: The Passion and the Legacy by Randell L. Makinson, Gibbs Smith, 1998.

Illustrated Mission Furniture Catalog, 1912–13 by the Come-Packt Furniture Company, Dover Publications, 1991.

In the Arts & Crafts Style by Barbara Mayer, photos by Rob Gray, foreward by Elaine Hirschl Ellis, Chronicle Books, 1992.

Lifetime Furniture, reproduction of circa-1910 catalog, Philmont, NY: Turn of the Century Editions, 1981.

Limbert Arts and Crafts Furniture: The Complete 1903 Catalog, by Charles Co. Limbert, Dover Publications, 1992.

The Mackintosh Style: Design and Decor by Elizabeth Wilhide, Chronicle Books, 1998.

Mission Furniture: Furniture of the American Arts and Crafts Movement, Schiffer Publishing, Ltd., 1997.

Quaint Furniture in Arts and Crafts, New York, New York: Turn of the Century Editions, 1988.

Roycroft Furniture (1906 catalog reprint), New York, New York: Turn of the Century Editions, 1981.

Roycroft Furniture catalog, 1906 by the Roycrofters, New York: Dover Publications, 1994.

Stickley Craftsman Furniture Catalogs by George Stickley, Gustav Stickley, L. Stickley and J.G. Stickley, Dover Publications, 1979.

Stickley Style: Arts and Crafts Homes in the Craftsman Tradition by David M. Cathers and Alexander Vertikoff, Simon & Schuster, 1999.

Style: 1900, published quarterly, 333 North Main Street, Lambertville, NJ 08530, www.ragoarts.com.

The Mission Furniture of L. & J.G. Stickley, New York, New York: Turn of the Century Editions, 1989.

The Arts & Crafts Price Guide: Gustav Stickley, Roycroft and L. & J.G. Stickley, Treadway Gallery, Inc., www.treadwaygallery.com, 1998.

Limbert Furniture, Philmont, New York: Turn of the Century Editions, 1997.

index